Conversations with God

Also by Sharon Swain and published by SPCK:

Christian Assemblies for Primary Schools [1995]
More Christian Assemblies for Primary Schools [1998]
The Sermon Slot: Ideas for All-Age Worship Year 1 [1992]
The Sermon Slot: Ideas for All-Age Worship Year 2 [1993]

CONVERSATIONS WITH GOD

Fifty Dramatic Dialogues
to Bring the Old Testament Alive

———

Sharon Swain

First published in Great Britain in 1999 by
Society for Promoting Christian Knowledge
Holy Trinity Church, Marylebone Road
London NW1 4DU

British Library Cataloguing-in-Publication Data
A catalogue record for this book is available from the British Library

ISBN 0–281–05151–8

Scripture references made to Good News Bible
(Today's English Version), published by Bible Societies/HarperCollins,
© American Bible Society, New York, 1966, 1971, 1976

Photoset by Wilmaset Ltd, Birkenhead, Wirral
Printed in Great Britain by
The Cromwell Press, Trowbridge, Wiltshire

Contents

CONTENTS

Introduction

In the pages of the Old Testament we read how the people of a small tribe living in the Middle East, thousands of years ago, started a two-way relationship with God. He was generous as well as jealous; they were rebellious and sometimes disloyal. Yet somehow the relationship grew and developed, despite numerous setbacks.

The story of how the Creator of the world made himself known to men such as Abraham, Isaac and Jacob is the greatest of all stories. But in their conversations with the Almighty surely they would have used the language and idiom of their day; they would have argued and fought with him as they sought to understand his commands; and as God surely has a sense of humour, they would have laughed with him.

Conversations with God looks at the exchanges between some of the people in the Old Testament and God, and allows us to imagine what might really have been said in the language of our time. Perhaps they echo the kinds of conversations we have today in the privacy of our hearts with a loving and jealous God.

How might these conversations be used? In worship, they could follow the actual reading of the Old Testament or stand on their own, perhaps as a prelude to a sermon. Alternatively they could be used in the Family Service or during a school assembly; with adults or with children.

Ideally, the person reading the part of God should be 'off stage', that is, out of sight, and they could be male or female. The Old Testament character should be 'on stage', but seen in profile, perhaps kneeling. The words can be read from the script. They do not have to be learnt.

The conversations should be read at some speed, with a snappy but natural style. It is also essential that each word can be heard clearly by all present. Use could be made of a telephone, as a prop, if desired. If there is any difficulty over saying unfamiliar names, encourage the actors to say them in a way that is comfortable for them, and to practise them until they can be said easily.

These conversations should be fun, as well as informative – so enjoy them!

Sharon Swain
1998

1

Adam tries to explain

Genesis 3

GOD   [*sadly*] Why, Adam? Why?

ADAM   Why, God?

GOD   Yes! Why, Adam?

ADAM   Why what?

GOD   [*patiently pursuing*] Why are you wearing clothes?

ADAM   [*innocently*] Well, why not? It gets quite chilly at night in Eden, after all.

GOD   Chilly in Eden?

ADAM   Yes! You didn't make it quite as perfect as you thought, you know.

         [*Getting into his stride*]

         And as for walking around the garden with all those plants – well, I ask you!

GOD   Well, what?

ADAM   Prickly!

GOD   Prickly?

ADAM   Definitely prickly!

GOD   What *are* you talking about, Adam?

ADAM   The plants are very prickly when you've got no clothes on! I would have thought you would have realised that when you made them!

GOD   Ah, I see. Prickly.

         [*Pause*]

         Is there anything else wrong?

ADAM   Well, it's a little monotonous eating only fruit. Have you tried eating fruit every day? Definitely does something to the stomach.

GOD   Fruit. Ah, yes. Anything else?

ADAM   No, I don't think so. If there is, I'll let you know.

GOD   Well, perhaps you'll listen to me now.

ADAM   [*airily*] Well, I haven't much time. I've still got to find somewhere for Eve to sleep tonight. It's far too cold to sleep outside in the garden. Do you suppose any of the trees would be suitable for thatching?

GOD   Trees for thatching? Why, in the Garden of Eden, do you *want* a thatch?

ADAM   [*as if to an idiot*] To cover the roof of the house! Why else? We have to have somewhere to live, you know. It just isn't done to live in the open, without even a tent. What would the neighbours say?

GOD   You haven't got any neighbours, Adam.

ADAM   Well, that's beside the point. Without a roof we'll get wet when it rains.

GOD   It's Eden, for goodness sake!

ADAM   You mean it doesn't rain? I don't believe it. Anyway, Eve won't live outside any longer, she needs her own home.

GOD   Adam?

ADAM   [*continuing unabated*] And if Eve wants a home, she gets one. There's no living with her when she gets into one of her moods.

GOD   [*irritated*] Adam!

ADAM   [*still continuing*] So, are there any trees I could use to roof the house?

GOD   [*very irritated*] Adam! Will you please listen to me?

ADAM   What? Oh, OK, I'm listening! What is it?

GOD   Did I, or did I not, give you one instruction when I put you into this garden?

ADAM   [*thinking*] Did you? I can't remember.

GOD   You can't remember?

ADAM   Well, it seems to me that you gave me a number of orders. Which was the most important one?

GOD   Not to eat from the tree of knowledge of good and evil!

ADAM   Which tree was that? They all look much the same to me, you know. I'm not a gardener. Now Eve, she knows all the names and fruits of each tree in the garden.

GOD   Exactly!

ADAM   [*suddenly understanding*] Oh, was it *that* tree?

GOD   Yes!

ADAM   Well, I couldn't help it. Eve gave me the fruit. It wasn't my fault.

GOD   And you just ate it?

ADAM   Well, what am I supposed to do, check everything she gives me to eat? I'd never hear the end of it.

GOD   So it's all Eve's fault, is it?

ADAM   [*hesitating*] Well, no, not really.

GOD   What do you mean 'not really'?

ADAM   It was the serpent's fault!

GOD   [*sarcastically*] Oh, so now we're going to blame it on the snake, are we?

ADAM   Well, he was hanging around at the time!

GOD   None of this was your fault, I suppose?

ADAM   [*pause*] Well—

GOD   You aren't to blame at all?

ADAM   [*slowly*] Well, I suppose I did know that we weren't to eat the fruit of this tree.

GOD   Thank you! Now can we start again, now that we've got the truth at last?

2

Cain and God

Genesis 4

GOD   What *is* the matter with you? Why are you scowling?
[*Laughs*]
You know what they say about the 'wind changing'?

CAIN   It's no joke! And what do you mean, 'what's the matter with me'? You know perfectly well what's the matter with me, God!

GOD   I do?

CAIN   [*shouting*] Yes! You do!

GOD   Then tell me about it.

CAIN   Why did you do that to me?

GOD   [*mildly*] Do what to you?

CAIN   [*shouting*] Will you stop that – copying everything I say!

GOD   Was I?

CAIN   You humiliated me in front of my brother and the whole of the family. How could you do that to me?

GOD   Your brother came offering me a sacrifice – the best of his lambs.

CAIN   [*still angry*] And I came offering my sacrifice – the best of my harvest produce.

GOD   With one major difference.

CAIN   What difference? We both made our harvest offerings to you, as we've always done at this time of the year. What difference is there between this year and the last? What difference is there between both of us?

GOD   Your brother came in innocence. He came to please me.

CAIN   [*sulkily*] My brother always pleases you.

GOD   And so do you, when you do what is right—

4

CAIN   [*to himself*] That *would* be a miracle, these days!

GOD   [*continuing*] Those who come to worship in sincerity will always be welcome in my presence.

CAIN   [*still sulkily*] I don't know what you mean!

GOD   [*continuing*] Those who come to me, not to confess, but with evil still alive in their hearts, will never be welcome in my presence.

CAIN   But you know we are mortal men, Lord.

GOD   True. All that lives, dies.

CAIN   No, I mean, you know we cannot live up to your standards.

GOD   *Are* my standards so very difficult?

CAIN   Difficult? They're impossible! No-one is ever going to manage to keep them. You ask too much of us.

GOD   [*mildly*] Others manage to keep them.

    [*Pause*]

    Your brother keeps my laws.

CAIN   [*crossly*] My brother is a saint!

GOD   [*ironically*] True, very true.

CAIN   But you ask too much of *me*, Lord!

GOD   Do I?

CAIN   Yes! I've tried! I've really tried!

GOD   Not very hard.

CAIN   [*crossly*] You don't understand!

GOD   Oh, yes, I do. I understand perfectly.

CAIN   [*very cross*] No, you don't! How could you understand? Have you lived in my family? Have you seen how my brother has been favoured from birth – how his words are hung on, how his gifts are accepted by our father, how his jokes are welcomed?

GOD   And does not your mother favour you?

CAIN   [*grudgingly*] Perhaps she does, a little.

GOD   And are you not the elder son? The son who will inherit from your father?

CAIN   [*grudgingly*] Yes, I suppose so.

GOD   Then why are you so jealous of your younger brother?

CAIN   [*sulkily*] He's always so *perfect*!

GOD   [*very sternly*] Where *is* your brother at this moment?

CAIN   [*guiltily*] How on earth should I know where he is? Have you looked out on the hillside? He's probably gone off to the winter pastures to look after his precious sheep.

GOD   He's not there.

CAIN   Then try the milking shed, he's probably cosseting one of his cows. That's all he ever seems to do.

GOD   He's not there, either.

CAIN   [*airily*] Then I really don't know where he is. Why come asking me? Am I my brother's keeper?

GOD   [*sternly*] What have you done to your brother? What terrible thing have you done to your brother, Cain?

3

God's instructions to Noah

Genesis 6.5–21

GOD   Noah, I'd like a moment of your time.

NOAH   What's that? Hang on a minute.
[*Speaking to someone else*]
Yes, Shem, I'll be with you in a moment. Ask your mother what she thinks about us going out with the boys tonight. You know what a fuss she made last time.

[*Turning his attention back to God*]
What was that, God?
[*Answering his wife now*]
Now, dear, you know we couldn't help it last time. I promise we'll be back early.

GOD   [*mildly*] Shall I come back to you a little later, when things are less busy?

NOAH   What? Oh, no. It's all right – just a small domestic problem. I think I've sorted it now.

GOD   [*ironically*] Sounds to me as if your wife's sorted it.

NOAH   [*amused*] Well, yes, you're probably right. Anyway, sorry about all that. What was it you wanted?

GOD   I wanted to chew an idea over with you, really.

NOAH   [*enthusiastically*] Oh, great! Chew away!

GOD   Well, to be honest I've more or less made up my mind, actually.

NOAH   Fine! What is it?

GOD   I've got a job for you. There's something I want you to build.

NOAH   [*very enthusiastically*] Great – what is it? A house, a table – I'm pretty good at tables. It's become my speciality recently since the daughter-in-law saw the one I made for the wife.

GOD   [*patiently*] Noah, I don't want a table, I don't want a chair, I don't even want a house – I want a boat.

NOAH   [*surprised*] A boat? Well that's a strange thing to want. Where on earth are you going to sail it? There's nothing round here to sail it on. We're a long way from the sea.

GOD   *I* don't need it, Noah. But *you* will.

NOAH   *I will*? Well, I'm sorry to tell you, Lord, that you're wrong there. If you think I'm going to trek to the nearest stretch of water to sail a boat, when I get sea-sick just looking at water, you've got another think coming. And can you

7

imagine what the wife would say if I just upped and disappeared? She's bad enough when I want to go out with the lads for an evening, she'd never let me go for a few weeks.

[*Continuing with hardly a breath*]

Besides it's lambing time, and you know what that's like—

GOD   [*raising his voice above Noah's voice*] Noah! When you've quite finished, perhaps you'd listen to me!

NOAH   [*apologetically*] Oh, sorry, God! It's just been one of those days. Go on, I'm listening now.

GOD   There's going to be a flood – a bad one – and I want you to build a boat large enough to take you and your family – together with as many animals as you can collect.

NOAH   A flood? How do you know there's going to be a flood?

[*Silence*]

Oh, sorry, I forgot who I was speaking to.

GOD   [*continuing*] The boat must have three decks, with a roof and a door on one side, and you'll need to line it with tar, to keep the water out.

NOAH   Can't I leave it until later in the year, when we've finished lambing? It's a really difficult time at the moment.

GOD   [*ruthlessly continuing*] You've got exactly seven days, and in that time you've got to stock it with food for a long voyage, and fill it with every kind of animal you can catch.

NOAH   Seven days?

[*Flatly*]

It's impossible!

GOD   That's all the time you've got before the rains start to fall.

NOAH   The rains? I thought you said it was a flood.

GOD   It's going to rain non-stop for forty days, until nothing is left on the earth.

NOAH	[*pausing*] You mean everything will drown? But what about the people?
GOD	Yes! What I have created I will destroy!
NOAH	[*shocked*] Everything you made is to be destroyed? But why?
GOD	I have seen how wicked the people are, and how they disobey my words.
NOAH	But, even so—
GOD	However, I will save you and your family, because you have obeyed my commands. I will also make an agreement with you, and you together with your family will be safe.
NOAH	[*suddenly decisive, shouting*] Shem, Ham, Japheth, I need you, *now*. We've got work to do!

4

But why, God?

Genesis 9.9–17

NOAH	God!
	[*Pause*]
	Are you there?
GOD	Yes, Noah, I'm here.
	[*Pause*]
	I'm always here, you know.
NOAH	Well, I know that but sometimes I forget.
GOD	I've noticed! But you're not the only one to forget.
NOAH	[*pause*] Can I ask you something?

GOD   Of course.

NOAH   It's about the flood.

GOD   Yes?

NOAH   What was it you said the other day, about the *bow* in the sky?

GOD   [*sighing*] You weren't listening *again*.

NOAH   Well, I was, but you see everything was wet – and it took so long to dry the clothes – and Shem was impatient to get away, and—

GOD   [*interrupting*] In other words, you weren't listening!

NOAH   [*shamefacedly*] No, sorry. So what *was* it you said?

GOD   I said that I'll never destroy all the living creatures on the earth again, and as proof of my promise to you I will put a bow in the sky, so that when it rains you will know that I've not forgotten my promise.

NOAH   [*awkwardly*] Excuse me, but what's a *bow*?

GOD   A rainbow.

NOAH   Yes, but what *is* a rainbow?

GOD   [*sighing*] A coloured arc that stretches from one side of the sky to the other.

NOAH   [*still not understanding*] Oh.

        [*Pause*]

GOD   Was that all?

NOAH   [*slowly*] No, not really, I wanted to ask you about why you did it.

GOD   What?

NOAH   Why you killed everyone. I mean, they can't all have been bad, can they? What about the babies and young children?

GOD   You haven't been listening again, have you?

NOAH   [*sheepishly*] Probably not.

GOD   *I* made this earth and all its people, and as the Creator surely I can destroy it if I want to?

NOAH   [*doubtfully*] I suppose so – but couldn't you just have made people better?

GOD   [*indignantly*] Better? How could I make you *better*? Do you want four arms, or another head?

NOAH   [*amused*] No, I didn't mean that. I meant, couldn't you have made them *nicer* people?

GOD   Oh, I see what you mean. Well, I couldn't have done that either.

NOAH   Why on earth not?

GOD   [*patiently*] Because I gave you all free will.

NOAH   But what's that got to do with it?

GOD   [*as though to a small child*] Because you have free will you can choose to be good or evil. I can't make you *all* nice. You're not puppets.

NOAH   [*thinking*] So in other words you're saying it was all our fault, then?

GOD   Yes, I thought you knew that.

NOAH   Well, I suppose I did really. But how do we know we can believe you this time?

GOD   Have I ever broken a promise before?

NOAH   [*thinking*] No, I don't think you have.

GOD   Well, then, you'll have to trust me.

NOAH   [*almost to himself*] That's easier said than done.

GOD   Pardon?

NOAH   Nothing.
[*A second thought*]
But how do we know you care for us – you say you do, but Ham still broke his leg, and Japheth fell down the gangplank, and now he can't walk properly.

GOD   Whose fault was that?

NOAH   Oh, all right, it was mine – I moved the ladder.

GOD   There you are, then. You can't blame it all on me.

NOAH   No, but—

11

GOD   [*impatiently*] But, but, but! I can't always protect you. Can you, as a father, always stop your children getting hurt?

NOAH   No, I suppose not.

GOD   And would you want to anyway?

NOAH   No – they've got to learn for themselves.

GOD   That's right, and they have to make their own mistakes. That's the way they'll learn.

NOAH   All right, I believe you care for us, but I still have some questions I want to ask you about—

GOD   Stop! Stop! That's enough! Make a list of the questions you want to ask me. I'm exhausted.

NOAH   Right! That's just what I'll do!
[*As if writing it down*]
'If God cares for us, why is it that—'
[*His voice tails off*]

5

Where do you want me to go?

Genesis 12.1–5

ABRAM   God?

GOD   Yes, Abram. What do you want?

ABRAM   Did I dream it, or did you ask me to go to Canaan?

GOD   You didn't dream it. I did suggest you might go there.

ABRAM   [*indignantly*] *Suggest* I go there! As I remember it, you practically ordered me there!

GOD   [*mildly*] Did I? Well, that's not how I remember it. It's not my habit to *order* people to do anything.

ABRAM   Maybe you don't think of it as *ordering* people about, but it's a pretty strong person that ignores your *suggestions*, isn't it?

GOD   Perhaps you're right, Abram. But it's still your choice, you don't have to do as I ask.

ABRAM   Well, all right! Now about this *suggestion* of yours. Firstly, where on earth is Canaan?

GOD   [*airily*] It's south, over the mountains of Lebanon.

ABRAM   [*suspiciously*] Hang on a minute! How far away is it?

GOD   [*casually*] Oh, it's not far, really. A few hundred miles, I suppose.

ABRAM   You call that *not far*? When did you last walk this area, with its mountains and valleys, its bandits and warring tribes?

GOD   [*slightly offended*] Well I may not have walked it, but I do know what it's like.

ABRAM   And that's supposed to keep me happy is it, that you 'know what it's like'? Remember what you said when we left the city of Ur?

GOD   Can't say I do, particularly.

ABRAM   You made me leave my comfortable home, in my civilised home town, and drag all my family, *including* my father, to Haran. 'It'll be a good move for you,' you said, 'much better than staying in Ur.'

GOD   Well, hasn't it been a good move for you?

ABRAM   [*sarcastically*] Oh, sure! My father Terah's just died! Maybe if we'd stayed in Ur he'd still be alive.

GOD   [*positively*] Well, you're halfway to your destination, and it's time you moved on once more.

ABRAM   [*resignedly*] How am I going to tell Sarai that we've got to move again? She's only just got settled into the new house.

GOD   [*not very interested*] That's up to you, Abram.

ABRAM   And living in tents again! You know she hates that.

13

GOD   [*tentatively*] Try telling her 'God says it's time to move'.

ABRAM   [*laughs*] Oh, yes! Can you imagine what she'd say to that? I've never lived down the last time. 'God says we've got to leave Ur', I cheerfully said all those years ago as we sat on the patio one warm evening under the stars. Boy, was I naive in those days.

GOD   [*mildly*] Well, it was only a suggestion.

ABRAM   [*ignoring God's interruption*] She's reminded me of my statement every single day since. When we got stuck in the river, she reminded me! When we ran out of food in the desert, she reminded me! When the animals all died, she reminded me—

GOD   You *could* tell her that Canaan is the *Promised Land*!

ABRAM   [*stopping in his tracks*] The what?

GOD   The Promised Land.

ABRAM   [*suspiciously*] And what's that – sounds like a sweet for a child!

GOD   [*evasively*] It's the land I've – prepared – for my people to live in.

ABRAM   [*still suspicious*] What do you mean 'prepared for us to live in'?

GOD   [*avoiding the issue*] Look, I promised to make you the Father of a Nation, didn't I? And a nation has to have somewhere to live. Canaan is a good place to grow food and bring up children. It has rich soil, grapes and olives grow in abundance. It's a land of milk and honey!

ABRAM   [*still slightly suspicious*] All right, if it's that good it would be worth going. But it still doesn't solve the problem of how to tell the family.

GOD   I'm sure you'll find a way.

ABRAM   [*beginning to think about going*] I could suggest we need a bigger place to bring up the family, what with my nephew Lot and all his people—

14

GOD   [*mildly*] You're going to Canaan, then?

ABRAM   Well, since you're *suggesting* and not *ordering* me to go to Canaan, I might as well give it a try. Now where did we put those tents?

6

God's promise to Abram

Genesis 15

GOD   [*calling*] Abram! I'd like to talk to you!

ABRAM   Yes, God? What is it?

GOD   You've done very well! I'm pleased with all you've achieved recently.

ABRAM   Great! Thanks for that. It's good to hear.

GOD   [*continuing*] Yes! You've done really well.

ABRAM   [*earnestly*] I couldn't have done it without you, though, Lord. There were times when I thought we'd certainly bitten off more than we could chew.

GOD   [*amused*] Like taking on four kings at the same time. Most would be happy with one king!

ABRAM   All for the sake of Lot.

GOD   Nevertheless you've done well, and because of this I shall make a promise to you. In future I will continue to keep you safe from danger.

ABRAM   I might well need that promise if my nephew Lot gets into any more trouble.

GOD   I trust not from any more local kings.

ABRAM   [*reminiscing*] What a distance we had to go – all the

	way to Damascus. I thought they'd never stop running! We nearly caught them outside the village of Dan, after I divided the men into groups and attacked them at night, but in the end they fled even further north.
GOD	And still you managed to rescue Lot and his family, bringing them back safe and well.
ABRAM	As well as making an alliance with the king of Salem.
GOD	Good work!
ABRAM	He's one of your priests, I gather. It'll be good to have an ally around here. It feels less threatening.
GOD	Melchizedek's a good man.
ABRAM	[*pause*] Was there anything else?
GOD	Yes – I intend to give you a reward.
ABRAM	[*offhand*] Oh, thanks.
GOD	You don't sound very grateful. You don't even know what it is, yet.
ABRAM	Well, a reward's not much good to me, is it? I've got all I need.
GOD	[*amazed*] Got all you need?
ABRAM	Yes – sheep, goats, even a wife! I've got no-one to pass it on to after all, have I?
GOD	There's always Eliezer.
ABRAM	True. He's my heir, and he means a lot to me, but ultimately he's a slave. He's not one of my own kind, is he?
GOD	You needn't worry, Eliezer won't inherit your wealth. You shall have a son of your own.
ABRAM	[*amused*] So Sarai's going to have a child, after all these years of marriage? Nice one, God! Some hopes!
GOD	You don't believe me?
ABRAM	It's not her fault. I know she can't have children, but I love her too much to dissolve our marriage.
GOD	You don't believe me.

ABRAM	Well, it's not that, I'm just facing facts.
GOD	Look up into the sky – what do you see?
ABRAM	What?
GOD	[*insistent*] Look up into the night sky. What is there to see?
ABRAM	[*looking*] Well, there's, the stars, and—
GOD	Can you count them?
ABRAM	[*startled*] What?
GOD	Can you count the stars at night?
ABRAM	No! Of course not! They're far too many to count!
GOD	[*making a statement*] So shall your descendants be.
ABRAM	My descendants?
GOD	[*continuing*] And for their inheritance they will have land from the border of Egypt as far as the River Euphrates.
ABRAM	To have descendants, I need to have a son.
GOD	Exactly!
ABRAM	[*amazed*] Truly? I will have a son?
GOD	You will have a son. You will also live to a good old age, and you will die in peace.

7

God can do anything

Genesis 18.1–15

SARAI	God?
	[*Pause*]
	Are you there?
GOD	Yes, Sarai.

SARAI   I'm glad about that.

GOD   I'm always here if you call me, Sarai.

SARAI   Yes, sorry, I forgot.

GOD   [*patiently*] What do you want?

SARAI   [*hesitantly*] Were you joking when you told Abram that I would have a son? I mean you didn't *really* mean it, did you?

GOD   I wasn't joking, Sarai.

[*Pause*]

I'm not really known for being a practical joker, am I?

SARAI   No, no, you're not. Though I've sometimes wondered, well, I mean, well, anteaters and giraffes? Seems to me that anyone who can make animals like those must have something of a sense of humour.

GOD   [*musing*] Perhaps you're right.

[*Pause*]

You were asking me about your son—

SARAI   [*trying to do this delicately*] Yes, my son – you *do know* how old I am, don't you, God?

GOD   [*patiently*] Yes, Sarai, I do know how old you are. You're, let me see—

[*As though counting on fingers*]—you're, seventy, no, is it eighty? Well, you're old enough, anyway.

SARAI   Exactly! I'm far too old to have children. It's simply not possible for me to have a child. And look at Abram. He's ninety-nine years old. Whoever heard of someone who's nearly a hundred fathering a baby?

GOD   I admit it's difficult, but it certainly isn't impossible.

SARAI   [*getting carried away with her argument*] And as for knowing if it's a boy or a girl, well only God could do that!

GOD   [*mildly*] Exactly.

SARAI   [*remembering to whom she is speaking*] Oh, sorry! I forgot who you were. But you know what I mean.

GOD   I know what you mean, Sarai.

SARAI   Now if it had been forty or fifty years ago that would have been different, but just to drop by and tell me that in nine months I shall have a baby, well it's, it's quite ridiculous.
[*Getting carried away again*]
Can you imagine what Lot and his family would say. They'd surely laugh at us.
[*Getting further carried away*]
Oh, yes! And what on earth does Abram want with this 'Father of a Nation' idea. He should be settling down to retirement, putting his feet up and letting Lot get on with looking after things, not trekking across the country looking for a 'Promised Land'.

GOD   [*mildly*] Is *that* how you feel, Sarai?

SARAI   [*defiantly*] Yes, I do!

GOD   [*patiently*] Fine.

SARAI   [*after a moment*] Is that all you're going to say, 'Fine'? Aren't you at least going to argue with me?

GOD   No, I don't think so. Do I need to argue with you, Sarai?

SARAI   Well, it's all right for you. But Abram's an old man.

GOD   Is he complaining, then?

SARAI   [*loath to admit the truth*] Well, no, I suppose he's not. He thinks it's wonderful.

GOD   So he believes what I've told him?

SARAI   Oh, yes! He'd believe anything you say.

GOD   And what about you? What do you believe, Sarai?

SARAI   [*thinking about it, slowly*] Well, I do know that you can do anything.

GOD   Yes.

SARAI   Even give us a child at our age, can't you?

GOD   Yes.

SARAI   And make Abram the father of a whole nation, with as many descendants as the stars in the sky. That *is* what you said, isn't it?

GOD   Yes.

SARAI   [*coming to a definite decision*] You're quite something, God, you really are!

GOD   [*smiling to himself*] Thank you, Sarai. So are you.

8

Abraham pleads with God

Genesis 18.16–33

GOD   Abraham, I've got something important to tell you.

ABRAHAM   Hang on! Could you just wait a minute, I'm rather busy.

GOD   [*not amused*] Rather *busy*! Do you know who you're talking to?

ABRAHAM   Yes, of course – God! It's just I'm saying goodbye to some visitors. I won't be a moment.

GOD   [*acidly*] Then I suppose I must wait, since the rules of hospitality can't be ignored, can they?

ABRAHAM   Of course not!
          [*Pause*]
          Right! Now what can I do for you? They've gone on their way, now.

GOD   So glad you've a moment free.

ABRAHAM   [*amused*] Now don't sulk – they were your messen-

	gers, so it was only fair that I gave them a decent farewell.
GOD	[*sulkily*] God never sulks!
ABRAHAM	No? Really?
GOD	No.
ABRAHAM	[*changing the subject*] Your messengers took me to look at the town of Sodom, this morning.
GOD	That's what I want to talk to you about.
ABRAHAM	Sodom?
GOD	Well, Sodom *and* Gomorrah.
ABRAHAM	What about them?
GOD	I've heard reports that they're evil places, filled with wicked men and women.
ABRAHAM	I've also heard about them. In fact everyone around here knows what they're like. I can't say I'd wish to live in either city, though to be fair they may not be as bad as we've heard.
GOD	My messengers will find out the truth.
ABRAHAM	And what then? What can be done about them?
GOD	What do you think?
ABRAHAM	Well, I suppose you could, well, you could—
GOD	If the accusations are correct, you mean I could destroy them?
ABRAHAM	Well, you could, but would you really want to destroy both towns, out of hand?
GOD	I don't know about 'out of hand', but if the reports are true – if the people are as evil as I have heard – then, yes, I would do so.
ABRAHAM	[*worried*] But what if some of them aren't evil? Surely they can't all be the same? Perhaps there are some good people in these cities.
GOD	[*cynically*] If there are, I haven't heard of them!
ABRAHAM	But what if there are say, fifty good people living

	there. You surely wouldn't destroy these cities, in case you killed *them*?
GOD	Wouldn't I?
ABRAHAM	But if they're innocent! How can you kill them? They may have children, wives and grandparents. They may be trying to live a good life despite the wickedness of those around them.
GOD	They will be tarred with the same brush. You cannot live so close to evil and escape it.
ABRAHAM	Yes, you can! Noah remained true to you, even though everyone else was evil!
GOD	That's true.
	[*Pause*]
	Perhaps you're right, Abraham. Possibly my messengers will find some good people in these cities.
ABRAHAM	Then if they find fifty good people, you will save both cities?
GOD	[*pause*] All right! If we can find fifty people who are not evil in Sodom and Gomorrah, I will not destroy either cities.
ABRAHAM	But, but, what if—
GOD	But, but, but – I know exactly what you're thinking, Abraham. What if there are only forty-five good people, or thirty-five good people, or twenty-five good people? Just where do you think I'm supposed to stop?
ABRAHAM	God, forgive me, but you are a God who protects the innocent. Please protect them now. If you find ten good people, save them!
GOD	Because *you* ask, Abraham, and you are a good man, I will save the cities if I find ten good people living in them.

22

ABRAHAM	Let us hope your messengers report back favourably, then, Lord.
GOD	Let us hope so.

9

You can't mean it, God!

Genesis 22.1–14

GOD	[*calling*] Abraham! Abraham!
ABRAHAM	[*answering, not very surprised*] Yes.
	[*Pause*]
	Is that you, God?
GOD	Of course! Who else do you think it could be?
ABRAHAM	[*amused*] No-one! It's just that I wasn't expecting you.
GOD	[*patiently*] But I thought you were praying?
ABRAHAM	Well, I was, but I didn't expect you to answer me.
GOD	[*interested*] So what *do* you think prayer is all about?
ABRAHAM	[*thinking*] It's rather like a conversation between two people, a bit like Isaac and I speaking to each other.
GOD	'A conversation between two people'—
ABRAHAM	Yes.
	[*Pause*]
	What are you getting at?
GOD	When you and Isaac speak to each other you both talk, it's not a one-sided affair, is it?
ABRAHAM	No, of course not.

23

GOD	So why should our talk be one-sided? Why should you speak and I remain silent?
ABRAHAM	I see what you mean. [*Pause*] I don't allow you to do much talking, do I?
GOD	Not often. You remind me of your wife, Sarah. She never allows you to get a word in edgeways, either!
ABRAHAM	[*smiling*] Yes, she does go on a bit, doesn't she? All her family are like that – they never stop talking. They always—
GOD	[*interrupting, patiently*] Exactly!
ABRAHAM	Oh, sorry! There I go again, not letting you get a word in edgeways. What did you want?
GOD	I have a task for you.
ABRAHAM	[*cheerfully*] Fire away, then. What can I do for you?
GOD	[*business-like*] I want you to take Isaac, your beloved son and go to Moriah—
ABRAHAM	[*interrupting*] No problem! When do you want me to go? Will tomorrow be early enough for you?
GOD	[*still continuing*] I will show you exactly where to go – it's on a mountain-top – and—
ABRAHAM	[*still cheerful, interrupting*] That's all right, then. We'll set off tomorrow morning. I can't think why you want me to go at this time of the year when all the sheep are lambing and there's so much work to do. Still you're God, and who am I to argue?
GOD	[*flatly*] And offer Isaac as a sacrifice to me!
ABRAHAM	[*not hearing God*] If you were to ask me to walk barefooted to Haran, I'd do it. Just ask, and it's yours— [*Suddenly realising what God has said*] What did you say?
GOD	Offer Isaac as a sacrifice.

24

ABRAHAM	[*pause*] You *are* joking, aren't you?
GOD	Am I?
ABRAHAM	[*determinedly continuing*] What do you really want me to do? Come on, ask me and I'll do it. I can't say fairer than that, can I?
GOD	Offer Isaac.
ABRAHAM	[*confused*] But why? You told me that I was to be the 'Father of a Nation', and that my descendants would be as numerous as the stars.
GOD	I did.
ABRAHAM	But how can that happen, if Isaac is to die? I only have one son, and I'm too old to have another. [*Laughs ironically to himself*] What am I saying – how can I kill my son? Surely you can give me another task? I'll do anything else you want.
GOD	A few moments ago you were offering to do *anything*. There were no strings attached to your promise, then.
ABRAHAM	Yes, but Isaac, my beloved son?
GOD	Fine! You don't want to do what I ask – that's your decision.
ABRAHAM	Well, it's not that I don't want to do what you ask, but—[*sudden thought*]—what would Sarah say?
GOD	So Sarah is more important than your God?
ABRAHAM	[*pausing to think*] No. [*With gathering confidence*] No, she's not more important to me than you.
GOD	So you will go to Moriah with Isaac?
ABRAHAM	[*quietly*] Yes. [*Pause*] I don't begin to understand your reasoning, but I do trust that you know what you're doing. If you say I shall be the Father of a Nation, then I shall be.

25

[*Pause*]
All right! I'll leave my future *and* my beloved son's
future in your hands.

10

Jacob and Esau

Genesis 31–33

JACOB   God? Are you there?

GOD   Yes, Jacob?

JACOB   Oh, hang on! A problem's come up. I'll be back in a
minute!
[*Pause*]

GOD   Jacob? Are you there, Jacob?
[*Total silence*]
Jacob, will you answer me? I thought you wanted to
speak to me.
[*Pause*]

JACOB   Sorry, Lord. It was Rachel and Leah, again.

GOD   If you *will* marry two wives!

JACOB   [*irritated*] And *whose fault* was that?

GOD   Well it was hardly mine, was it?

JACOB   And certainly not mine! You know full well it was my
father-in-law's idea, because he thought his elder daugh-
ter should be married before the younger.

GOD   Well, you could have stopped there, couldn't you?

JACOB   How could I?

GOD   One wife was surely enough!

JACOB   But I loved Rachel. It was Rachel that I wanted to marry all along.

GOD   In that case you'll have to put up with the problems of two wives, won't you?

JACOB   Thanks a lot for the sympathy!

GOD   Oh, was *that* what you wanted?

JACOB   No, not exactly. But it would have been nice.

GOD   Sorry, I didn't realise that's what this was all about.

JACOB   It wasn't really.

[*Pause*]

I wanted to speak to you about something else that's on my mind.

GOD   Fire away, then! What is it?

JACOB   It's about the suggestion you made to me.

GOD   Suggestion?

JACOB   Yes, you know.

GOD   Which suggestion?

JACOB   That I should leave my Uncle Laban and the land of Mesopotamia, and go back to my father's land of Canaan.

GOD   Well, things have been difficult recently, haven't they?

JACOB   True. We're never going to agree over which goats and sheep belong to Laban, and which belong to me and my family.

GOD   So the suggestion to leave is a good one?

JACOB   Er, no.

GOD   You're not leaving for Canaan, then?

JACOB   I'm not sure at the moment. You see, there's a *slight* problem.

GOD   There is?

JACOB   Yes, my brother, Esau.

GOD   What's wrong with Esau? There's nothing wrong with him.

JACOB   I don't know.

      [*Irritated*]

      No! I don't mean that! I haven't seen him for years, after all.

GOD   So what's the problem? He'll be pleased to see you.

JACOB   [*to himself*] He'll probably kill me.

GOD   What's that?

JACOB   [*louder*] He'll kill me.

GOD   [*laughing*] Nonsense! Of course he won't.

JACOB   [*earnestly*] I'm not joking. He'll kill me.

GOD   Do stop repeating yourself, it gets monotonous.

JACOB   I'm telling you, Esau will kill me if I return to Canaan.

GOD   Why?

JACOB   You know why! I stole his blessing from our father – his birthright – which meant everything to him. He tried to kill me once before.

GOD   He didn't. He planned to, but he didn't carry it out.

JACOB   [*getting carried away*] That's what you think! If I return I'm done for, and he'll probably kill my wives and children after dealing with me.

GOD   Rubbish! He'll do such thing!

JACOB   You don't know my brother. He's got a temper, and a few years won't have made any difference. In fact, it might have made him worse.

GOD   Well, it seems to me you'll just have to go and find out if I'm right, unless you want to stay here.

JACOB   Thanks! Most encouraging! In other words I've just got to trust you. That's what you're saying, isn't it?

GOD   Yes.

JACOB   You're not asking much, are you?

GOD   No.

JACOB   Great!

GOD   You've always trusted me in the past.

JACOB	That's true.
GOD	So it's no different, is it?
JACOB	No.

[*Pause*]

OK! You win! I'll take Rachel, Leah and the children and go back to Canaan. *And* I'll trust you that Esau wants peace between us.

11

Doubting God

Genesis 32.22–32

JACOB	Right, God! I've sent my wives and children over the river before me.
GOD	[*mildly*] So I see, Jacob.
JACOB	*And* all my sheep and cattle. Everything's gone across the River Jabbok.
GOD	So you said.
JACOB	So now we can talk in peace and quiet, without anyone else around – man to man as it were.

[*Pause*]

[*Laugh*]

Or rather man to God, I suppose.

GOD	Go ahead then. What is it? You've got something to say, I see.
JACOB	A number of things to say, really, and it's more than time you and I got together, don't you think?
GOD	[*mildly*] I'm always here. You only have to turn my way.

JACOB   Yes, well! That's easier said than done, isn't it? By the
        time I've dealt with both my wives – with Rachel and
        with Leah; kept the peace between the children; decided
        where to stop for the night; given orders to strike camp;
        and sorted out any squabbles, I'm not left with much
        time for myself, am I, never mind finding time to speak to
        you!

GOD   [*ironically*] Such a busy life you lead, Jacob! I'd no idea!

JACOB   [*a little ashamed*] Well, I'm sure your life is busy too – I
        was only trying to explain that I can't always speak to
        you when I might want to.

GOD   [*thoughtfully*] Perhaps it depends on how much you *want*
        to speak to me, Jacob.

JACOB   Yes, well, you might be right! But I *am* talking to you
        now God, so let's get on with it!

GOD   Proceed then, Jacob.

JACOB   [*hesitating*] Well, this might seem a rather silly question
        in the circumstances—

GOD   Go on.

JACOB   But how do I know you *are* God? [*Hurriedly*] I mean you
        could be anything – a figment of my imagination, or my
        conscience, or—

GOD   Yes?

JACOB   [*running out of ideas*] Or, er, well, I don't know! But you
        know what I mean! How do I know that you are – as you
        say – the *one* God?

GOD   [*mildly*] Perhaps because I say I am?

JACOB   Oh, really!
        [*Pause*]
        But that's not really good enough. After all I could *say*
        I'm the leader of a large tribe of people, but it doesn't
        mean that I necessarily am.

GOD   [*ironically*] You *have* got quite a big tribe!

30

JACOB   [*preening himself*] Not bad really, is it?
        [*Suddenly cross with himself*]
        Oh, don't get me side-tracked! Answer my question, please.

GOD   [*amused*] It doesn't take much to side-track you, Jacob, does it?

JACOB   [*still irritated*] Come on, answer me!

GOD   What's the question again?

JACOB   You know perfectly well. How do I know you're *actually* God?

GOD   I'm not sure you're going to like this Jacob – but as I've said – the answer is because I say I am.

JACOB   Oh, this is getting us nowhere. Why can't you give me some proof that you're this Almighty God – the *one* God?

GOD   If I did, you'd still not necessarily believe me, would you?

JACOB   Of course I would!

GOD   Well, what about the dream you had on the road to Haran, at the place you decided to call Bethel?

JACOB   But that was such a long time ago—

GOD   [*interrupting*] What did you promise me that day?

JACOB   [*trying to remember*] Something about, if you protect me, and if I return safely home, then you would be my God—

GOD   Exactly! Not much wrong with your memory, is there after all, Jacob? And what did I offer in return?

JACOB   [*thinking*] You would give me this land – and my descendants would be as numerous as the specks of dust on the earth.

GOD   You believed me, then, Jacob, why do you doubt me now?

JACOB   Things are different now!

GOD   How?

JACOB   [*gloomily*] I've got to go and meet Esau.
        [*Pause*]

He's got hundreds of men—
[*Pause*]
I don't know how he's going to greet me.

GOD   You're afraid.

JACOB   [*pause*] Yes! He's no reason to wish me well. After all I cheated him out of his birthright once.

GOD   But that was many years ago.

JACOB   [*gloomily*] He won't have forgotten, I'm sure.

GOD   Neither have I forgotten, Jacob.

JACOB   What?

GOD   My promise stands for ever.

JACOB   [*understanding*] You really *are* God, aren't you?

GOD   Haven't I said so?

JACOB   *My* God!

GOD   As I said.

JACOB   And wherever I go you'll be there to protect me.

GOD   Yes, definitely!

JACOB   [*apologising*] I guess I'd forgotten for a moment.

GOD   [*as if reading from an agreement*] I will protect you. Your people will be my people, and I will be your God.
[*Solemn announcement*]
From this day forward your name is not Jacob, but Israel, for you have struggled with me, and won.
[*Formal blessing*]
Go in peace, Israel!

12
The decision
Genesis 34—35.15

GOD   Jacob! Jacob!
[*Pause*]
Jacob! Are you listening?

JACOB   Yes! Who is it? What do you want?

GOD   *Who is it?* Who do you *think* it is? I thought you'd come out into this desert to *be with me* – to talk to me?

JACOB   Oh, sorry, God! I didn't realise who it was. I thought it was one of the children come to fetch me back to Rachel.

GOD   Well, now we've got it clear that Rachel doesn't need you, can we start again?

JACOB   [*rather flippantly*] Yes, of course! Carry on, don't mind me!

GOD   [*coolly*] I wasn't.
[*Pause*]
If you're quite ready perhaps *I* can speak now.

JACOB   Go ahead, I'm listening. I'm all ears!

GOD   [*more to himself than Jacob*] Well, that makes a change!

JACOB   What is it? Can I do anything for you?

GOD   [*ignoring this*] It's time for you to move on.

JACOB   [*gloomily*] Don't I know it. We've outstayed our welcome here that's for sure.

GOD   Exactly! It's not very safe, is it?

JACOB   About as safe as living on top of a volcano, I'd say.

GOD   [*chuckling to himself*] Personally I'd rather live on the volcano, I think!

JACOB   I might have guessed that Simeon and Levi would overreact, but they could have stopped short of murdering half the Canaanites in the area.

GOD   They only wanted to protect their sister Dinah's reputation.

JACOB   Well her reputation was already protected, wasn't it? After all Shechem had agreed to make amends for carrying off Dinah and was willing to marry her. What's more he'd offered a good bride price. She was settled for life. We'd never have to worry about her again.

GOD   By marrying out of her own tribe?

JACOB   [*thoughtfully*] Yes, well I didn't think you'd be too happy about that.

GOD   You're quite right, I'm not!

JACOB   But now we're about to be set on by all the tribes in the area because of the murder of Hamor, and his son, Shechem.

GOD   So you're ready to move on?

JACOB   Are you suggesting we should?

GOD   I'm asking the questions – but it's time that *you* decided what you really want to do.

JACOB   What do you mean, '*What I want to do*'?

GOD   Just what I said – what do you want to do? Do you want to settle here and intermarry with the other tribes in Canaan, and become another branch of the Canaanite people, worshipping their gods, eating their food, and marrying their women?

JACOB   [*slowly*] I'm not sure that sounds a very good idea, especially the bit about becoming a 'branch of the Canaanite people' and 'worshipping their gods'.
[*Having second thoughts*]
Although as for 'marrying their women'—

GOD	[*interrupting quickly*] Let's leave that on one side for the moment.
JACOB	Well, what's wrong with marrying their women? They produce strong, healthy women in this area, you know!
GOD	[*dryly*] Most attractive too, from what I've seen.
JACOB	[*excitedly*] I should say so. I saw the most beautiful woman yesterday—
	[*Remembering he is talking to God*]
	—Well, never mind about that now!
GOD	The choice is yours. It's time for you to decide about the future. You can stay here in Canaan and lose your own identity, or you can truly become my people.
JACOB	[*a little warily*] What do you mean 'become your people'? You promised my father and grandfather something of the sort. But not a lot seems to have happened since then.
GOD	[*interrupting*] Because they disobeyed me. They turned their back on me, and ignored my wishes.
JACOB	Sounds typical of my father!
GOD	So first, a test. I want you to go to Bethel with all your family, and build an altar to me. You are to instruct your family to get rid of their foreign gods, to put on clean clothes and to worship me, the God of your fathers.
JACOB	Some tall order!
	[*Pause*]
	All right, I'll give it a go!
GOD	[*making a pronouncement*] From now on your name is to be Israel, not Jacob. On you I will build many nations, and I will give you the land which I gave to Abraham and Isaac.
JACOB	[*regretfully*] But no Canaanite women! Oh well, it was only a dream!

35

13

Dreaming for a purpose

Genesis 37

JOSEPH   God?

[*Pause*]

God, are you there? I've got a little problem.

[*Pause*]

God? Where are you?

GOD   Yes, Joseph, what is it?

JOSEPH   I think I've made a mistake.

[*Pause*]

Well, one or two mistakes, really.

GOD   [*ironically*] Really! You don't say?

JOSEPH   [*seriously*] Yes, really!

GOD   Go on, what have you done wrong?

JOSEPH   Well, you know the dream I had a few days ago.

GOD   Which one was that – the one about the sheaves of wheat?

JOSEPH   No, the other one.

GOD   Ah! The sun, moon and stars?

JOSEPH   Yes, that's the one. I dreamt that the sun, moon and stars all bowed down before me.

GOD   What about it? Did you finally decide what it actually meant?

JOSEPH   [*diffidently*] Well, that's the problem. I thought it meant that my father, mother and brothers would one day bow down to me.

GOD   [*non-committally*] Really!

JOSEPH   [*defensively*] Well, what else was I supposed to think?

GOD	[*interested*] Do you always say exactly what you think to your family, Joseph?
JOSEPH	Usually, why ever not?
GOD	[*dryly*] It could be why you're always in trouble. People don't really like such honesty, you know.
JOSEPH	[*flippantly*] Well that's their problem, isn't it? It's not mine.
GOD	Seems to me it's often your problem as well.
JOSEPH	[*gloomily*] It certainly is this time.
GOD	Tell me.
JOSEPH	As you know I've never really got on with my step-brothers. They've always been jealous of me, because my father loves me more than them.
GOD	He also loves your brother Benjamin, I think.
JOSEPH	Yes, he does. It's because our mother was his favourite wife.
GOD	[*pausing to wait for Joseph to speak*] Yes?
JOSEPH	[*puzzled*] What?
GOD	I thought you were going to tell me about your little problem?
JOSEPH	Oh, yes, sorry, I forgot. My problem. [*Groan*] And, boy, is it a problem!
GOD	Go on.
JOSEPH	I'm in a hole – a huge hole!
GOD	A hole? [*Suddenly enlightened*] You mean you're in another jam of some sort?
JOSEPH	[*irritated*] No, of course not – well I am really, but that's not what I meant. Call yourself God and you don't know what's actually happened?
GOD	Sorry, but you did say you were in a *hole*.
JOSEPH	Yes, but I mean a real hole – a hole in the ground. My

	brothers have tied me up and left me in this hole in the ground. I've been here all night, and I'm cold and tired.
GOD	[*amazed*] Why on earth have they put you in a hole?
JOSEPH	I told you, I annoyed them by telling them about my dreams—
GOD	Is that all? Goodness, what would they do if you really did something bad?
JOSEPH	*And* they didn't like my coat!
GOD	[*not sure he understands*] What?
JOSEPH	My coat – the one my father gave me. My wonderful coat with its long sleeves, and the pattern around the bottom. It makes me feel like a king.
	[*Pause*]
	But really I think it was the dreams. I wish I'd not told them now, but kept them to myself.
GOD	Your dreams are important—
JOSEPH	[*interrupting*] They sure are if they get me into this much trouble.
GOD	But you need to use them to *help* people, not upset them—
JOSEPH	That's all very well, but how am I to get out of this hole – and survive?
GOD	Oh, you'll be getting out of there shortly, and then those dreams of yours will be very useful. So keep practising the interpretations.

14

To speak or not to speak

Genesis 39.20—40.23

JOSEPH   God, there's something I need to talk over with you – something I need to get clear, really.
           [*Pause*] Are you there?
           [*Pause*] Are you listening, God?

GOD   I'm here!

JOSEPH   For a minute I thought you'd left me. That wouldn't have been good news, at the moment.

GOD   It wouldn't?

JOSEPH   [*with feeling*] Definitely not.

GOD   You don't say!

JOSEPH   [*irritated*] You don't say? Is that all the comment you can make? Here I am in prison, with no likelihood of getting out for the foreseeable future, and all you can mutter is 'You don't say'!

GOD   I thought you were doing all right there.

JOSEPH   [*ironically*] Oh, yes! I'm fine – I'm just fine! I was sent here by Potiphar because of his wife's lies, and here I'm likely to stay for the next dozen years. No-one gets out of jail in Egypt, unless it's feet first!

GOD   You always were given to exaggeration.

JOSEPH   Thanks for the support!

GOD   Anyway, I thought that the chief jailer was a fan of yours.

JOSEPH   He is.

GOD   He's put all the other prisoners in your charge, hasn't he?

JOSEPH   That's right, he has.

GOD   So things aren't so bad, then?

39

JOSEPH   Well, I suppose they're better than they could be – I'm not in the darkest dungeon, or on bread and water. But now how about listening to my problem?

GOD   What problem's that?

JOSEPH   To tell, or not to tell.

GOD   Pardon?

JOSEPH   Should I tell him or not?

GOD   Joseph, would you like to explain what you're on about, in more detail?

JOSEPH   OK! OK! Here goes! The captain of the guard has put two prisoners in my charge.

GOD   So what's new?

JOSEPH   Nothing special in that.

GOD   So?

JOSEPH   So these two have had dreams.

GOD   [groan] Oh, not again! Haven't you had enough to do with dreams?

JOSEPH   They certainly seem to follow me around, don't they?

GOD   You can say that again.

JOSEPH   So the question, as I said, is should I tell them or not?

GOD   What the dreams mean?

JOSEPH   Yes!

GOD   What do you think?

JOSEPH   That's what I'm asking you, God.

GOD   Oh, so you were.

JOSEPH   The cup-bearer dreamt of a vine with three branches. On the branches were grapes, and he took the grapes and pressed them into Pharaoh's cup.

GOD   Interesting.

JOSEPH   Good news, isn't it? He's going to be restored to his position as Pharaoh's cup-bearer.

GOD   What about the other prisoner?

JOSEPH   The chief baker.

GOD	What about his dream?
JOSEPH	He dreamt that he was carrying three baskets of bread on his head, and the birds came and ate from the top basket full of bread.
GOD	Oh, dear!
JOSEPH	Exactly!
GOD	Not so good, is it?
JOSEPH	No!
GOD	So, what will you do?
JOSEPH	That's the problem. What can I do? How can I tell him that Pharaoh seeks his life?
GOD	Whether you tell him or not, it will come to pass.
JOSEPH	As I said, things are not good here.
GOD	You might try asking the cup-bearer to help you when he's free. He might remember that you tried to help him when he was in prison.
JOSEPH	Nice one, God! I'll do that! I knew you'd have something helpful to say.
GOD	Glad to be of service, Joseph. Give me a buzz next time you want help.
JOSEPH	I will, you can be sure of that.

15

Jacob goes to Egypt
Genesis 46

GOD	Jacob! It's all right! I've got the messages, you can stop!
JACOB	Who's that? Who's there?

GOD	Stop offering sacrifices! I've got the message!
JACOB	Who is it?
GOD	[*irritated*] *Who is it?* You've been offering sacrifices to me at Beersheba for days. Who is it, indeed!
JACOB	Is it *you*?
GOD	Is it *who*?
JACOB	The God of my fathers – the God of Abraham and Isaac?
GOD	Who else?
JACOB	The God who appeared to them and promised that they would be the—
GOD/ JACOB	[*together*]—Father of a Nation!
GOD	Exactly!
JACOB	[*pause*] Well you've been remarkably quiet recently, haven't you?
GOD	Have *you* tried to speak to me in the last few months, Jacob?
JACOB	[*embarrassed*] Well, life has been a little hectic, you know! What with Joseph, and—
GOD	Ah, yes, Joseph.
JACOB	After all these years, he's come back.
GOD	I know.
JACOB	It's wonderful! He turned up in Egypt as Pharaoh's right-hand man. Amazing!
GOD	I know.
JACOB	All this time when I thought he was dead, when I thought a wild animal had killed him, instead he was safe in Egypt.
GOD	[*heavily*] I know.
JACOB	[*amused*] I know! [*Laughing*] Of course you do! You're God!
GOD	So, what is it you want? You obviously want something,

coming to Beersheba and offering sacrifices to me each day.

JACOB   I needed to ask you something. I'm not sure whether I should go to Egypt, or not. The boys seem to think it would be best if we all moved to live near Joseph.

GOD   You don't think so?

JACOB   I'm not sure. You once said to me that, well, that I would be the Father, well—

GOD   The Father of a Nation, exactly!

JACOB   You meant it, then?

GOD   [*sarcastically*] No, I usually say things I don't mean.

JACOB   Sorry, but I just wondered whether you'd forgotten what you'd said. After all nothing much seems to have happened since then, does it?

GOD   So you assume because things have been quiet recently, I've forgotten my promise. Oh, Jacob! How foolish you are!

JACOB   I'm sorry, Lord. It's sometimes hard not to have doubts.

GOD   So I noticed.

JACOB   Also, well, I wondered, well—

GOD   Yes, Jacob?

JACOB   Well, you'll probably think it's silly.

GOD   I promise you I won't.

JACOB   Well, I wondered if you would stay with us.

GOD   [*astonished*] If I'd *stay* with you? Where did you think I'd go?

JACOB   No, I didn't mean that exactly!

GOD   Well what did you mean, *exactly*?

JACOB   I wasn't sure if you'd still be with us if we went as far away as Egypt.

GOD   I'm not tied to Canaan, Jacob, if that's what you mean.

JACOB   Well, I wasn't sure. Perhaps you only lived here.

GOD   I will be with you wherever you go. I am with you in

Canaan, and I will be with you in Egypt. I will also bring your people back to Canaan in the future, and make of them a great nation.

JACOB   Then we shall go to Egypt together, Lord.
GOD   Amen to that, Jacob. Amen.

16

What's your name?

Exodus 3

GOD   Moses!
MOSES   [*startled*] Who's that?
GOD   Moses, come here!
MOSES   What?
GOD   Come over here! Come on! This way!
MOSES   [*still puzzled*] Who is it? Where are you?
GOD   Here! Come nearer to me.
MOSES   But who are you?
GOD   I am the God of your ancestors – the God of Abraham, Isaac and Jacob.
MOSES   [*impressed*] Gosh!
    [*Pause*]
    But where *are* you?
GOD   Over here.
MOSES   Hang on! I'm coming.
GOD   Stop! Just a moment.
MOSES   Make up your mind, either I'm to come over there, or I'm not.

GOD First you must take off your shoes. This is holy ground.

MOSES What do you mean 'holy ground'? Don't be silly! It's just ground.

GOD [*warning*] Moses!

MOSES Oh, all right, I take that back.

[*Scared*]

What are you doing? I'm getting out of here. There are flames coming out of a bush, but it's *not burning*! That's impossible!

GOD Don't be afraid.

MOSES [*to himself*] Don't be afraid, he says. It's all right for him – but whoever heard of a bush in flames that doesn't burn. I don't like it, not one bit!

GOD Moses! Are you listening?

MOSES Listening? Yes, I can hear you. But I'm not looking.

GOD Why on earth have you covered your face?

MOSES I'd rather not look. You never know what might happen. I don't want to upset you, God, but I'd rather not look at you. However, do go on – keep talking.

GOD I have a task for you.

MOSES A task? What is it?

GOD I have heard the complaints of my people. I have seen how cruelly they have been treated by Pharaoh.

MOSES Tell me about it!

GOD I will rescue them from the slave-drivers.

MOSES Wonderful! About time. What are you going to do?

GOD I'm not going to do anything—

MOSES [*succinctly*] Then how *are* you going to rescue your people? This should be interesting.

GOD [*continuing without listening to Moses*] —*you are*!

MOSES What did you say?

GOD You're going to get them free!

MOSES [*gloomily*] That's what I thought you said.

45

GOD   No problems!

MOSES   You *must* be an optimist, that's all I can say, if you think I can get the Israelites free. Pharaoh is not going to let them go!

GOD   He *will* set my people free!

MOSES   But I can't go to the king. I'm no-one. How can I go to Pharaoh and demand that he frees the Israelites? He'll just laugh at me.

GOD   You won't be on your own.

MOSES   [*ironically*] Oh, yes! And what idiot is going to come and share my fate!

GOD   I am. I will be with you every step of the way, Moses.

MOSES   [*awkwardly*] Yes, well, that's fine, but I'd rather have someone else – no, I mean I'd like to have another *man* with me.

GOD   [*dryly*] I think you might be better off with me, Moses.

MOSES   And when I speak to the Israelites, what am I supposed to say to them?

GOD   That I have sent you to them to free them.

MOSES   [*laughing*] That won't be enough. They'll want to know who has sent me. I can't just say 'God sent me'.

GOD   I don't see why not. Surely that's enough?

MOSES   They'll want to know your name, at the very least, I should think. And what will I say to that?

GOD   Tell them my name is 'I AM', or if you prefer, 'Yahweh'. I am the one who has sent you to them. Tell the Israelites that I am the God of their ancestors, of Abraham, Isaac and Jacob, and I have sent you to free them from their slavery.

MOSES   [*pause*] And if I do get them free? Where are they to go?

GOD   You are to lead them to Canaan – the land that I have prepared for my people.
      [*Pause*]

My people *will* listen to you.

MOSES   [*pause*] And Pharaoh will free them?

GOD   Yes – eventually.

17

Power from God

Exodus 4.1–17

MOSES   I've been giving some thought to what you said the other day, God.

GOD   [*ironically*] Amazing! Well done, Moses!

MOSES   [*ignoring this*] It's all very well for you to tell me to go to the Israelites and get them to tell Pharaoh that they want to be free.

GOD   What's wrong with that? It's a simple enough instruction, isn't it?

MOSES   Oh, yes, perfectly simple! But do you really think the Israelites will obey me, or for that matter will believe the words actually came from you?

GOD   I don't see why not! Haven't you spoken to them yet?

MOSES   [*emphatically*] No! What if they don't believe me?

GOD   They will.

MOSES   I really don't see how you can be so sure.

GOD   [*laughing*] No, you probably don't. Just trust me, Moses, the people will obey you, at least over this.

MOSES   It's all very well for you to laugh, but I'm the one who has to go and speak to them.

GOD   Well, perhaps I can help.

MOSES   [*sceptically*] How?

GOD   Throw down the stick you are holding, onto the ground in front of you.

MOSES   [*pause – then a yell*] Get me out of here. It's not enough to give me impossible jobs, but now my stick turns into a snake!

GOD   [*shouts*] Moses! Don't run away, just trust me!

MOSES   [*to himself*] Oh, brilliant! *Trust him*, he says, when there's a snake about to attack me!

GOD   Now pick up the snake in your hand – preferably by its tail.

MOSES   [*grumbling to himself*] Now I'm expected to pick up the snake. Whatever next?

[*Pause*]

No, it's no good, I can't do it. I've never liked snakes, and I'm quite sure they don't like me.

GOD   Trust me, Moses. It will be all right.

MOSES   [*grumbling again*] Trust me, trust me! Has he got any idea what this is like?

[*Pause*]

GOD   There you see.

MOSES   [*jubilantly*] I did it! I did it! I really, really did it! I picked up a snake!

GOD   I told you.

MOSES   [*still amazed*] And now it's turned back into my stick. [*Slightly worried*]

It's not going to turn back into a snake again, is it?

GOD   [*laughing*] Not unless you throw it down before the people to convince them that the God of their ancestors, the God of Abraham, Isaac, and Jacob, has appeared to you.

MOSES   [*a little doubtfully*] Well, it might do the trick.

GOD   Do you want some more proof, Moses?

MOSES   [*anxiously*] Not really—

GOD   Put your hand into your robe, and then take it out – and again, once more.

MOSES   [*appalled*] My hand has turned leprous, it's pure white at the tips.

[*Pause*]

[*Amazed*] But now it's turned back to normal.

GOD   And if that will not convince them, then take some water from the Nile and pour it onto the ground. It will turn to blood.

MOSES   [*seriously*] God – I believe you. Stop! Please stop! Surely the people will trust you now, as I do.

18

The Nile turns to blood

Exodus 7.8–25

MOSES   God! Are you there?

[*To himself*]

I hope you are. I've got problems – not just *problems*, but *major* problems!

GOD   What is it, Moses?

MOSES   [*to himself*] He asks, 'What is it?'

GOD   Moses, you're muttering again. You must get out of the habit, it really is very annoying.

MOSES   Stop nagging me, Lord. It's worse than having a wife!

GOD   Thank you, Moses. Now, enough of this, what do you want?

MOSES   Well, we've done as you asked. Aaron and I went to Pharaoh to ask him to release our people, and as you thought, he immediately demanded a miracle.

GOD   So?

MOSES   I did as you said. I instructed Aaron to throw down my staff in front of the king.

GOD   And?

MOSES   Well, I can't say he was much impressed.

GOD   Oh?

MOSES   It's true, it did turn into a snake.

GOD   Yes?

MOSES   But he decided to call up all his court magicians.

GOD   Very clever!

MOSES   And you'll never believe it, but they managed do exactly the same thing. *All* their sticks turned into snakes.

GOD   That must have been fun! Mind you, I thought that might happen.

MOSES   However, our snake promptly ate up all the other snakes.

GOD   Good! That must have been a salutary lesson to Pharaoh.

MOSES   Not really. Pharaoh still refused to let our people go.

GOD   I warned you he might. Pharaoh is a very stubborn man.

MOSES   [*despondently*] We're never going to get away from Egypt. He's not going to release us, God.

GOD   Have patience, Moses, have patience. I've another plan.

MOSES   [*suspiciously*] What plan?

GOD   Don't rush me, Moses.

MOSES   Sorry.

GOD   Let me see.

         [*Pause*]

         In the morning, when Pharaoh goes down to the River

Nile you are to go there to meet him. Take your staff with you again.

MOSES   What then? Surely you can't do the same thing again? It'll be no good turning the staff into a snake again!

GOD   No! First, you are to ask him to let the people go in order that they can worship me in the desert.

MOSES   And after that? Because he'll still say 'No'.

GOD   After that you will tell him that he will learn that *I* am God Almighty, and I am going to teach him a lesson.

MOSES   And how is he going to learn that?

GOD   Tell him that he will learn who I am by what I shall *do*!

MOSES   [*pause*] And what will you do?

GOD   You'll see in due course.

MOSES   And if he still refuses?

GOD   If he still refuses you are to tell him that you will strike the surface of the water with the staff.

MOSES   [*amused*] What good is that, striking the water with a stick? If I produce a load more snakes, he'll just laugh!

GOD   [*deadly serious*] Warn him that the great River Nile, the greatest of all rivers in Egypt, will turn to blood.

MOSES   What!

GOD   Worse than that, all the fish in the river will die.

MOSES   Really!

GOD   And the river will stink so badly that the whole country will know of its death—

MOSES   Gosh! What will the people drink?

GOD   [*continuing*] They will not be able to drink from the river.

MOSES   Surely Pharaoh will listen then!

GOD   [*continuing*] Tell Aaron to hold the stick over all the rivers and canals in Egypt.

MOSES   And?

GOD   All will turn to blood!

MOSES   All the water in the land?

GOD   *All* the water in the land will turn to blood, unless Pharaoh lets my people go.

MOSES   [*slowly*] Surely, Lord, Pharaoh will let your people go now.

19

More plagues

Exodus 10.1–12

MOSES   [*wailing*] Lord! Lord! I'm at my wit's end! What on earth am I to do now?

GOD   *You* are at your wit's end!

MOSES   [*agitated*] I am, I am! What shall I do?

GOD   Will you calm down a moment, Moses, and cease your wailing.

MOSES   Wailing?

GOD   [*definitely*] Wailing! It's giving me quite a headache.

MOSES   [*crossly*] Well, it's all right for you to say 'calm down' but you're not having to deal with this king – this Pharaoh! I'm the one with the headache!

GOD   And I suppose I'm not the one that is having to deal with Pharaoh?

MOSES   No, you're not!

GOD   [*ironically*] I rather thought I was!

MOSES   I'm the one that has to meet him, and every time I go to him, he agrees to let us leave Egypt. Then he changes his mind.

GOD   Until another plague?

MOSES   Yes!

[*Pause*]

What on earth am I to do? I'm at my wit's end.

GOD   [*ironically*] You've said that once already. You're going round in circles.

MOSES   [*depressed*] I know.

GOD   Be more specific.

MOSES   Well, we've tried everything! After the flies, and after the hail Pharaoh agreed to let us go into the desert to worship you.

GOD   But?

MOSES   But it turned out that he only wanted to allow the men to go, and not the women and children. How could we leave them behind?

GOD   I told you he was stubborn.

MOSES   'Stubborn' isn't the word I would use for him. He's a—

GOD   [*interrupting swiftly*] Yes, yes, Moses! I agree, but calling Pharaoh names isn't going to help, is it?

MOSES   So what do you suggest?

GOD   Go to the king once more—

MOSES   And when he refuses, *once more*?

GOD   I will send another plague.

MOSES   Such as?

GOD   This time raise your hand over the fields of Egypt.

MOSES   [*sceptically*] And what good is that going to do?

GOD   [*almost to himself*] I wish you'd let me finish for once, Moses. It really is most irritating.

MOSES   Sorry. It's just that it doesn't seem as though we'll ever get away from Egypt.

GOD   I've told you already, you must have patience.

MOSES   I know, but patience isn't my strong point, as you may have noticed.

GOD   [*ironically*] No, I've never noticed!

MOSES   All right, I'll try to have patience.

GOD   Good.

MOSES   Anyway, what were you saying?

GOD   This time, raise your hand over the whole land of Egypt.

MOSES   And?

GOD   And a wind will come from the east.

MOSES   What good is a wind?

GOD   [*patiently*] The wind will bring locusts which will devour all the crops that the hail has left standing.

MOSES   Surely Pharaoh will hear our request then?

GOD   Let us hope so.

MOSES   And when the locusts come?

GOD   The land will be black with locusts. They will cover every living thing and no green plant will be left after they have passed.

MOSES   [*in awe*] There will be no food for anyone.

GOD   [*sombrely*] No food for anyone.

MOSES   And it will be a whole year before the storage barns are filled.

GOD   Pharaoh and his people have been warned.

MOSES   Surely, surely, Pharaoh will listen this time.

GOD   [*sadly*] Let us hope so, Moses.

20

Help, God!

Exodus 14

GOD   Were you calling me, Moses?

MOSES   Calling? I've been *yelling* for some time, God.

GOD   [*mildly*] It's not necessary to yell, I can hear you perfectly well, even when you whisper.

MOSES   [*still continuing*] In fact all of us have been calling you!

GOD   All of *who* [*to himself*] or is it *whom*?

MOSES   [*ignoring him*] All *your people*!

GOD   [*flatly*] My people only tend to call me when they need help.

MOSES   Yes, well, we need your help now.

GOD   I thought you might! What's wrong *now*?

MOSES   Everything!

GOD   *Everything*? Well that's different, usually it's one particular thing that's wrong.

MOSES   No, I mean, it's disastrous, and it's all your fault.

GOD   [*mildly*] I rather thought it might be, somehow.

MOSES   [*getting cross*] Well, you were the one who told us to leave Egypt. 'Go and tell Pharaoh to let my people go, and I will guide them to a better land', you said.

GOD   So what's wrong with that?

MOSES   Well, I told you I was no good at public speaking, and that Pharaoh wouldn't listen to me—

GOD   [*to himself*] You seem to be doing all right at the moment—

MOSES   [*interrupting*] And look what happened – we had plagues of frogs, and plagues of locusts, and plagues of boils, even – all because Pharaoh wouldn't listen to me.

GOD I rather thought it was because he wouldn't listen to *me*, actually.

MOSES Well, you know what I mean!

GOD [*patiently*] But the people of Israel did get away from Egypt in the end, didn't they?

MOSES Oh, yes! I'm not saying you didn't get us out of Egypt, or keep us safe, then.

GOD So what are you complaining about now?

MOSES Well, what on earth was the point in letting us leave Egypt if we're going to be slaughtered by Pharaoh's army out here by the Reed Sea?

GOD Oh, is that what all this is about?

MOSES [*very cross*] 'Is that what all this is about?', is that all you can say?

GOD [*wearily*] What else would you have me say, Moses?

MOSES [*angrily*] I don't want you to *say* anything, I want you to *do* something. Get *rid of them!*

GOD [*sadly*] You make me sound like some genie, or a magician, not GOD.

MOSES Well, I'm sorry, but things are too worrying to spend time soft-soaping you, God. Will you *please* help us, before it's too late?

GOD I see! Now you're asking my help?

MOSES Of course! What else did you think I was doing?

GOD I wasn't sure – moaning at me, I rather thought.

MOSES Will you help us, or you won't have a nation to look after in the future? The Egyptians are about to pound us into the dust.

GOD So I see.

MOSES Well—

GOD [*deliberate pause*] No.

MOSES [*almost squeaking in horror*] No?

GOD No.

MOSES	What are you playing at, God? You were the one who wanted us to leave Egypt. Was it just to kill us out here?
GOD	[*patiently*] I said, 'No, *I* won't help you' because you can help yourselves.
MOSES	[*sarcastically*] Oh, sure I can! What am I supposed to do – go out and face ten thousand Egyptian soldiers single-handed?
GOD	I have already given you the power to deal with Pharaoh's army. Haven't you learnt that yet?
MOSES	[*puzzled*] How?
GOD	[*patiently*] Lift the staff that I gave to Aaron, and hold it out over the sea. The water will separate and you can go over to the other side on dry land. Then see what will happen to any Egyptians who chase you!
MOSES	[*wearily, but believing*] Is that all I have to do? Well, why didn't you say so in the beginning—

21

No food!

Exodus 15.22—16.31

MOSES	[*somewhat nervously*] God?
	[*Pause*]
	God? Are you there?
GOD	Of course, Moses.
MOSES	[*with nervous laughter*] Well, of course you're there – you're always there, aren't you?
GOD	[*sighing*] What's the matter now, Moses?

MOSES   Well, nothing's the matter exactly – I just thought it was time we had a talk—

GOD   Did you? Well, that's nice.

MOSES   Yes, isn't it!

GOD   [*silence for a moment*]
Well, what would you like to talk about?

MOSES   Oh, this and that – you know.

GOD   Are you sure you haven't got something specific in mind?

MOSES   [*airily*] Well, nothing of *real* importance – just a little thing I wanted to ask you, if you've got the time. But it can wait, if you're busy—

GOD   Come on! Out with it!

MOSES   Well, if you're sure?

GOD   Moses! What is it? What are my people moaning about now?

MOSES   Well, it's quite understandable, really. I mean, you'd moan if you were in their position – to get them all the way out here and then, well, leave them in the lurch – so to speak! Not that I'm complaining really – but, well, it does seem a bit mean – and how much longer can they go without it, and—

GOD   [*interrupting*] Moses?

MOSES   [*innocently*] Yes, God?

GOD   What are you going on about?

MOSES   Well, I thought you knew?

GOD   Perhaps I do, but won't you tell me anyway?

MOSES   But why have I got to tell you if you know already?

GOD   Why does Aaron tell you what the people of Israel are saying, when you probably know their needs beforehand?

MOSES   [*thinking hard*] Because, well, well, he tells me so that I might be able to help.

GOD   Do you always wait to hear what Aaron says before you act? Or do you sometimes help the people without being asked?

MOSES [*still thinking it out*] No, of course I help the people without Aaron asking me to get involved. Sometimes I have to help them.

GOD But what about when Aaron comes saying, 'The people need your help, Moses'?

MOSES I try to help.

GOD And do you always give them what they want?

MOSES [*positively*] No, of course not! They often ask for such silly things. I mean, fancy wanting feather beds in the desert, or a three-course meal. Sometimes I have to say 'No'.

GOD But isn't that an answer?

MOSES [*thinking*] I suppose it is. But somehow we always expect an answer to be 'Yes'.

GOD So, now, will you tell me what the people of Israel want, and stop beating about the bush. I'm waiting to hear your request.

MOSES [*slightly embarrassed*] I'm sorry, God. It seemed wrong just to keep asking you for something.

GOD [*patiently*] But you're not asking for yourself, are you, Moses? You're asking for others. So tell me!

MOSES Well, it's like this – the people are so hungry, God, and thirsty. The only water we can find is sour, and it's made many people ill. Your people need your help fast if they are to survive.

GOD Well, why didn't you say so in the first place. Now here's what you should do—

59

22

The judges

Exodus 18.13–27

GOD   What's the matter, Moses? You look troubled.

MOSES   Oh, how did you guess?

GOD   How did I guess? What a silly question.

MOSES   Sorry, I forgot, you're good at guessing, aren't you, God?

GOD   Guessing? Really! If you've quite finished, Moses.

MOSES   Of course! Well, at least you've cheered me up.

GOD   [*dryly*] I'm glad I've achieved something. Now what's the matter?

MOSES   Well, it's Jethro.

GOD   Your father-in-law, Jethro? He came to join you last night?

MOSES   Yes.

GOD   And brought with him your wife and sons.

MOSES   Yes.

GOD   That surely can't be the problem? You were looking forward to seeing them again.

MOSES   [*enthusiastically*] True! It was great to see the boys again. How they've grown! I hardly recognised them.

GOD   So if it wasn't that, what was it?

MOSES   It was Jethro.

GOD   What's he done?

MOSES   Nothing. He's done nothing.

GOD   Then what is disturbing you?

MOSES   It's rather what Jethro *said* that disturbed me.

GOD   What he said?

MOSES   Yes.

GOD   When?

MOSES	This morning, when I was sorting out some of the disputes.
GOD	Which disputes? Who was fighting?
MOSES	No, not that kind!
GOD	Then, which kind of dispute?
MOSES	Arguments often occur between our people, and I'm called in to help settle them.
GOD	What's wrong with that?
MOSES	Nothing.
GOD	So why didn't Jethro like you settling problems among the people?
MOSES	Oh, he wasn't complaining.
GOD	So? Do get on with the story, Moses!
MOSES	[*ignoring him*] It was just that I sat listening to the people all day. [*Amused*] In fact the queue stretched right away out of sight.
GOD	You've obviously got a job for life!
MOSES	Well, that's the problem. Jethro's argument is that I shouldn't be spending all day listening to people's problems and laying down the law.
GOD	What's wrong with that? It's my law, after all?
MOSES	There's nothing wrong with it, according to Jethro.
GOD	I'm glad about that.
MOSES	[*amused*] Oh, he wasn't having a go at you, Lord. He's too good a man for that. He respects you.
GOD	I'm even more pleased about that. I was beginning to get fed up with 'Jethro says'!
MOSES	It's just he feels that, well, that I—
GOD	That you should what?
MOSES	[*slightly embarrassed*] That I should teach the people about you – about God.
GOD	Rather than judge their disputes?

MOSES Yes! Also, that I should instruct the people in the way that they should live.

GOD Then who will listen to their problems?

MOSES He thinks I should appoint some capable men and put them in charge of the people, making them leaders of thousands, hundreds, or tens of people.

GOD And what is wrong with that?

MOSES I'm not sure if this is the best way for us to go on in the future.

GOD Why not?

MOSES Should I be letting go of some of this work?

GOD Which is best for my people?

MOSES Well, that's the point. Which is?

GOD That there should be one leader who is too tired to do all the work? Or that there should be a number of judges, which will allow you to lead my people properly?

MOSES I suppose the judges can also bring any difficult cases to me.

GOD Of course.

MOSES So you think that this is good advice, God?

GOD What do you think, Moses?

MOSES [*pause*] I think it's good advice, Lord.

23

Mount Sinai

Exodus 19

GOD   Moses, do you think you could leave your work for one minute, and come and speak to me?

MOSES   [*preoccupied*] Yes.

[*Pause*]

In a minute or two.

GOD   I would rather like to speak to you *now*!

MOSES   Yes, *OK*! Give me a few minutes and I'll be with you! Just let me finish sorting out this—

GOD   [*interrupting*] Oh, now it's a '*few minutes*'. Well, perhaps you'll kindly come back to me *when* you're free, will you?

MOSES   [*distracted*] Yes, yes, of course I will!

GOD   I'm sure you'll find me in. After all God doesn't go out, does he? He's always on call.

MOSES   God? [*Aghast*] God? You didn't tell me it was *you*!

GOD   Well, who did you think it was? The old man of the mountain?

MOSES   [*amused*] No, one of *your people* wanting me, of course.

GOD   [*ironically*] Of course.

MOSES   Well, how was I to know? People call me all the time – all day and half the night.

GOD   Instead it's your God wanting you, Moses.

MOSES   All right, I've got the message! Don't read me the riot act.

GOD   [*amused*] Riot act, indeed! I only want to *talk* to you.

MOSES   Thank goodness for that.

GOD   However, I would like some peace and quiet, if possible.

MOSES   Why don't we go outside the camp?

GOD   Mount Sinai?

MOSES   Yes, we can talk as we go.

GOD   All right.

MOSES   [*pause*] What did you want to talk about?

GOD   [*pause*] You saw how I got you out of Egypt?

MOSES   [*enthusiastically*] I certainly did! No matter what Pharaoh tried, you won. He didn't stand a chance, did he?

GOD   [*mildly*] He could have agreed to let my people go when you first asked him, couldn't he?

MOSES   You said he was stubborn.

GOD   But you all came out of Egypt safely in the end.

MOSES   True! Thanks to you!

GOD   [*amused*] And you.

MOSES   It was great working with you, though I can't say I want to go through all those plagues again. Just thinking of the creepy-crawlies makes me feel itchy.

GOD   [*amused*] I know what you mean.

MOSES   So I trust there are no locusts around here.

GOD   [*blandly*] Not at present.

MOSES   I must admit I shall miss working with you.

GOD   Well, we could work together again.

MOSES   How?

GOD   If my people are willing to keep my commandments, and obey my laws, I will agree to be their God.

MOSES   [*unsure*] But I thought you were already.

GOD   What?

MOSES   Our God?

GOD   Of course I am. But I have something slightly different in mind.

MOSES   What do you mean?

GOD   The whole earth is mine and all its people.

MOSES   Of course.

GOD   However, in this case I was thinking that you and your people will be my *chosen* people – my *special* people.

MOSES   I don't understand.

GOD   Let me put it this way – although the whole earth is mine, I have chosen you out of all the peoples of the world to be *my* people.

MOSES   [*cautiously*] What would be involved?

GOD   A covenant.

MOSES   A what?

GOD   A covenant – an agreement between equals.

MOSES   Between equals, but you're God?

GOD   Between *equals*!

MOSES   Sounds amazing!
[*Cautiously*]
What would this covenant involve?

GOD   I will agree to be your God. And you and your people will be my people.

MOSES   You said that already. But what do we offer you?

GOD   You will obey my laws, and worship only me.

MOSES   Sounds good to me, but I must check whether everyone else agrees.

GOD   Good idea. We need everyone's agreement to make the covenant work.

MOSES   It will only work if we are *all* signatories to the covenant.

GOD   It will only work if everyone wants it to work. If everyone is prepared to make the agreement work, *then* it will be successful.

24

The golden bull

Exodus 32

GOD   [*urgently*] Moses! Are you there? Are you listening? Wake up!

MOSES   [*just waking up*] What? What is it? Who's waking me up?

GOD   Who do you think it is?

MOSES   Aaron, is that you? What on earth are you shouting at me for? Do be quiet, I've got a headache!

GOD   No, of course it isn't Aaron!
[*To himself*]
Shouting at you indeed!
[*To Moses*]
Aaron would hardly be up a mountain at this time of the morning, would he?

MOSES   [*amused*] No, I suppose not. He likes his bed too much.

GOD   Exactly!

MOSES   So who on earth has trekked halfway up a mountain to find me. It must be important. Come on, show yourself.

GOD   [*sadly*] Moses, Moses!

MOSES   [*getting irritated*] Oh, for goodness sake! Come out of the cloud so I can get a look at you!
[*Pause*]
[*Anxiously*]
Who is it?

GOD   Who do you think, Moses?

MOSES   Oh, it's you! I thought for a minute there'd been some major catastrophe and Aaron had come to fetch me back.

GOD   [*solemnly*] There has been a major catastrophe.

MOSES   [*not listening*] Last time I came up Mount Sinai, I'd only been here an hour when messengers came to call me back because the people were arguing about some order that Aaron had given them.

GOD   It hasn't changed much this time.

MOSES   [*suddenly hearing what God has said*] What was that you said?

GOD   I said, 'It hasn't changed'.

MOSES   What hasn't?

GOD   Your people.

MOSES   [*worried*] What's happened to them now?

GOD   Nothing's happened to *them*!

MOSES   Oh, that's all right then! You never know when I leave them, what might happen.

GOD   I said nothing's happened to *them*.

MOSES   So what's the matter, then? Why did you have to wake me up at this hour of the morning?

GOD   Because your people—

MOSES   [*interrupting*] Oh, they're now *my people*, are they?

GOD   What do you mean?

MOSES   Well, they're usually *your people*.
[*To himself*]
They *must* have done something wrong if they're *my* people.

GOD   When you've quite finished!

MOSES   [*flippantly*] Sorry.

GOD   As I was saying, *your people*, whom you led out of Egypt, have ignored my commands.

MOSES   [*now worried*] What on earth have they done?

GOD   They have sinned against me—

MOSES   [*interrupting*] Tell me!

GOD   [*continuing*]—and they have rejected me!

MOSES   [*shouting*] What have they done?

GOD   Your people melted down gold ornaments—

MOSES   [*shocked*] Oh, no!

GOD   Yes! Then they used the gold to make a golden bull!

MOSES   [*really shocked*] Oh, no!

GOD   [*irritated*] Stop saying, 'Oh no'!

MOSES   But surely they wouldn't?

GOD   [*grimly*] They have!

MOSES   [*nervous*] They haven't – you know?

GOD   Yes, they have! They have worshipped the golden calf which they have made, and offered sacrifices to it.

MOSES   But this is terrible.

GOD   They're even saying that this bull calf is the god who brought them out of Egypt.

MOSES   They can't be so gullible, surely?

GOD   It appears they can.

MOSES   Let me go down and speak to them. They don't know what they're doing, Lord.

GOD   I am very angry with them. I cannot forgive them.
         [*Pause*]
         I shall destroy them, and then I will carry out my promise to make you and your descendants into a great nation.

MOSES   [*pleading*] Please, forgive them, Lord.

GOD   No, I will destroy them!

MOSES   Don't forget the promises you made to my forefathers. You promised Abraham, Isaac and Jacob that you would care for them, that you would be their God and they would be your people.

GOD   In return for their obedience.

MOSES   Lord, please change your mind. Give them another chance.
         [*Solemnly*]

	Leave them to me, I will deal with them.
GOD	[*pause*] All right, I will not destroy them. I will leave you to punish them.
MOSES	Never fear, Lord, I *will* deal with them. They will not reject you again.
GOD	[*heavily*] We shall see. We shall see.

25

God's presence

Exodus 33.18–23

MOSES	God?
GOD	Yes, Moses, what do you want?
MOSES	It's some time since we spoke.
GOD	A few days.
MOSES	It seems longer.
GOD	Did you want something special, Moses?
MOSES	[*awkwardly*] No, not really.
GOD	Are you sure there's nothing you want to ask me?
MOSES	Well—
GOD	Yes?
MOSES	Can I ask you something?
GOD	Go ahead.
MOSES	[*nervously*] Well, it's a bit delicate, you see.
GOD	How do you mean 'delicate'?
MOSES	I don't quite know how to ask.
GOD	[*cheerfully*] Just ask.
MOSES	[*to himself*] That's easier said—

69

GOD	[*interrupting*] Moses, for goodness sake, what is it?
MOSES	Well, I hope you don't mind me asking—
GOD	[*to himself*] Well I won't know until you ask, will I?
MOSES	[*interrupting*] No, but—
GOD	[*irritated*] So go ahead. Go on!
MOSES	Well, I don't know—
GOD	[*brusquely*] Oh, do go on, Moses. Am I that terrifying?
MOSES	[*with feeling*] Most definitely. You want to try being me, instead of you. Then you'd understand!
GOD	[*amused*] Ask me what you want, Moses. Anything at all. Just ask.
MOSES	[*decisively*] OK, I will!
GOD	Yes?
MOSES	I wonder – can I *see* you? I want to know what you look like.
GOD	[*pause*] You have done well, Moses, and I am pleased with you. You have obeyed my words and my commands.
MOSES	So is the answer 'Yes'?
GOD	[*decisively*] Yes!
MOSES	Yes?
GOD	I will pass before you, so that you can see me pass by.
MOSES	That's wonderful!
GOD	But I will not let you see my face, that would be too dangerous.
MOSES	Why would it be dangerous?
GOD	All those who see my face, die. I would not wish to kill you, Moses, so I will take pity on you.
MOSES	Thank you, Lord.
GOD	I will also do something else. I will tell you my sacred name – a name that I give only to those who please me.
MOSES	[*overwhelmed – to himself*] I don't know what to say.
GOD	Come over here, Moses.

MOSES	Where, Lord?
GOD	Above you. There is a ledge on this rock-face.
MOSES	Where?
GOD	Up here.
MOSES	Here?
GOD	Yes. You will be safe standing here, in this crevice.
MOSES	What now?
GOD	When I pass by, my light will dazzle you.
MOSES	I'll close my eyes, then.
GOD	No, that still won't be safe. I will protect you by covering you with my hand until I have gone by.
MOSES	But how will I know that you have passed by me?
GOD	When I have gone by, I will remove my hand from you.
MOSES	And then what will happen?
GOD	You will be able to see my back.
MOSES	But not your face?
GOD	No, you would not be safe, and I do not want you to suffer. But you will be able to see me as I pass.
MOSES	I am your servant, God. I am honoured by this sign of your trust in me.

26

Going into Canaan
Numbers 13.21—14.25

GOD	[*angrily*] Moses! *Moses*, are you listening? I've had enough! I've absolutely had enough! To put it politely, I'm cheesed off!

MOSES   [*cautiously, puzzled*] Is that you, God?

GOD   [*crossly*] Well, who do you *think* it is? Do you usually hear other voices when you're praying?

MOSES   Sorry, I wasn't sure. You don't quite sound like your-self—

GOD   [*interrupting*] I'm not! I'm angry—

MOSES   [*continuing as though he's not heard*] —and things have been a little hectic here.

GOD   I know! That's why I'm going to take some action.

MOSES   [*alarmed*] Hang on! Things aren't that bad, really. I know the people have been a little restless recently, but things will calm down again if you give them a chance.
        [*To himself*]
        Well, I hope so.

GOD   Give them a chance? How many more chances do you expect me to give them?
        [*Getting into his stride*]
        How much longer will my people continue to ignore my wishes, and reject me? How much longer will they fail to trust me – despite all that I've done for them? How much longer—

MOSES   [*interrupting*] It's just that they think they're all going to die in battle. And they think that their wives and children will be taken away into slavery. You can't blame them, really.

GOD   [*still cross*] Can't blame them? Didn't I bring them safely out of Egypt? Haven't I looked after them all these years in the wilderness? Haven't I provided food and water when they were needed?

MOSES   Yes, but this is different. Canaan is full of fortified cities, and their men are *giants*.
        [*Gloomily*] They will surely destroy us.

GOD   Rubbish!

72

MOSES   And anyway what's the point – there's absolutely nothing worth having in Canaan.

GOD   [*stunned*] Nothing worth having in Canaan?

MOSES   The land is barren. At first we thought it might be quite fertile – the men we sent to spy out the land brought back oranges and pineapples – but the latest reports show that the country doesn't produce enough food even for its own people.

GOD   This is the *Promised Land*!

MOSES   Well, as Promised Land it doesn't promise much. And if that's not enough, the Canaanites are giants. How on earth are we supposed to defeat them?

GOD   Ah! Now we're getting to the truth.

MOSES   Caleb's men report that they're far too strong for us. We can't possibly defeat them!

GOD   And you believe Caleb?

MOSES   It's not a case of believing him. The people are about to choose a new leader—

GOD   [*interrupting, appalled*] *What*?

MOSES   —and return to Egypt!

GOD   *What*?

MOSES   [*patiently*] I wish you'd stop repeating everything I say, God!

GOD   Moses, didn't it occur to you to believe my words – that Canaan is the Promised Land – a land flowing with milk and honey?

MOSES   But they were so convincing – no fertile ground, and giants, that's what they said!

GOD   A fairy story told for gullible children.

MOSES   It was pretty convincing!

GOD   Really! I suggest you get Caleb to speak to his men again. You might find the real picture is a little different.

MOSES   [*pause*] Are you saying they didn't tell the truth?

GOD [*ignoring him*] What did Joshua, son of Nun, say? You sent him into Canaan, didn't you?

MOSES Yes, he's the only one who says the land *is* fertile. He's also sure that you will be there to help us if things go wrong.

GOD I'm glad someone trusts me.

MOSES He even tore his clothes—

GOD [*interested*] Really?

MOSES —in sorrow that the people were rebelling against your word.

GOD Most promising!

MOSES [*gloomily*] So promising that he nearly got himself stoned to death!

GOD [*sadly*] How much longer will my people rebel? How much longer will they fail to trust me?

MOSES They don't mean to rebel, you know.

GOD So what do you call going against my wishes?

MOSES I think it's rather that they're going against *my wishes*, if you see what I mean.

GOD That's the same thing, Moses, isn't it?

MOSES True, Lord.

GOD Nevertheless, I will take some action.

MOSES Be merciful, God.

GOD [*ignoring him*] Those who have disobeyed me will—

MOSES Don't kill them!

GOD —never enter the Promised Land.

MOSES [*relieved*] If you say so, God. If you say so.

27

Water from the rock

Numbers 20.1–11

MOSES   God! Did you get the message we sent you this morning?
        [*Pause*]
        God! Are you there?
        [*Pause*]
        Did you receive our message? It was rather urgent!

GOD   Moses. It's you again. What can I do for you now?

MOSES   [*getting irritated*] Did you get the message that Aaron and I sent you?

GOD   Message, what message? I seem to have received so many recently.

MOSES   About our water situation. We're desperate for water.

GOD   Just a minute, let me have a look.
        [*Pause*]
        Yes! Here it is. You're in the desert, at Kadesh, and as you say there's no water.

MOSES   [*patiently*] Well, can you help us? Things are pretty desperate. The people are complaining that we've brought them out here only to die.

GOD   [*sarcastically*] Do my people do anything else, other than complain?

MOSES   But at least they're not complaining about you this time.

GOD   That makes a change!

MOSES   But to be fair, God, it was you that called us to leave our homes in Egypt and follow you into this wilderness.

GOD   [*mildly*] I seem to remember that my people were only too keen to leave the fleshpots of Egypt.

MOSES   But at least Egypt had food. My mouth waters at the thought of all those pomegranates, grapes and figs.

GOD   But life wasn't all roses in Egypt, if I remember rightly.

MOSES   [*trying to be honest*] No, it wasn't, but we've forgotten about that after all the hardship of living in the desert. Egypt seems rather like the Promised Land now.

GOD   Pity you've all got such short memories! I seem to remember you were desperate to get away from Pharaoh and his slave-drivers then.

MOSES   [*trying to distract God*] Well, never mind that. Can you help us now? If we don't find water soon we'll all perish right here in Kadesh, and the Promised Land won't matter.

GOD   I would have thought the solution was in your own hands, Moses.

MOSES   [*crossly*] *In my own hands?* What do you mean?

GOD   Did I, or did I not, give you the power to use that staff of yours?

MOSES   My staff? Oh, yes, you did! I never thought of that!

GOD   Well, think of it now! Get Aaron to gather the people together, and then take your staff and strike the rock just where you're standing.

MOSES   [*sarcastically*] And what good is that supposed to do?

GOD   Just do it!

MOSES   And supposing nothing happens? Aaron and I will be in even more trouble!

GOD   Don't you think it's about time you trusted me, Moses?

MOSES   Trusted you? When you've led us into this dreadful place, where there's no food for us and our animals, and no water for us to drink. It might have been better to leave us in Egypt – at least we'd have died in our beds!

GOD   Moses—

MOSES	[*interrupting God*] It's not as if there'll be anyone to bury us out here in this God-forsaken place—
GOD	[*slightly amused*] God-forsaken?
MOSES	Oh, well, you know what I mean.
GOD	I *do* know what you mean! As I said, it's high time you trusted me!
	[*Pause*]
	Now are you going to stop complaining long enough to do what I ask?
MOSES	[*not listening*] What was that?
GOD	[*more to himself*] I knew you weren't listening! Gather the people together and then take your staff and strike the rock by you.
MOSES	[*gloomily*] And what good will that do?
GOD	The rock will gush water! It *was* water you wanted, wasn't it, Moses?
MOSES	[*grumbling to himself*] Water from a rock? Well, I've heard everything now!
GOD	[*getting very irritated*] Moses! Are you going to do as I say, or not?
MOSES	What, strike the rock? The people will think I've gone mad. Still I suppose if that's what you want—
GOD	It is!
MOSES	OK, I'll do it. I just hope it works.
GOD	It will.
MOSES	Well, you usually know what you're doing, I suppose.
GOD	[*gravely*] I do. I always know what *I'm* doing Moses.

28

The choosing of Joshua

Numbers 27.12–end

GOD   [*importantly, making an announcement*] Moses, the time is here.

MOSES   [*distracted*] What time is that, Lord?

GOD   It's time for you to *go*!

MOSES   [*even more distracted*] Go? Go where? I can't go anywhere at the moment, I've still got so many things to sort out – we haven't finished the last census, and there are still the inheritance laws to conclude. I never knew running a nation would mean so much work. And the—

GOD   Moses!

MOSES   [*pausing a second, but then continuing*] Then I must see about the offerings that we give at festivals—

GOD   [*shouting to get attention*] Moses! Will you stop this catalogue of busyness, and listen to me.

MOSES   [*rather irritated*] I *am* listening, God. What is it? I really am rather busy!

GOD   [*making a great pronouncement*] The time has come for you to go up Mount Abarim.

MOSES   [*stupidly*] Go up Mount Abarim?

GOD   I do wish you wouldn't keep repeating everything I say, it really is very irritating.

MOSES   Sorry, I didn't mean to, but you do come out with some strange things sometimes.

GOD   [*to himself*] I rather thought it was the other way around.

MOSES   OK, but where is Mount Abarim, and why have I got to

	climb it? I'm too old to climb mountains, you know! Why do you think I'm so busy – it's because I know I haven't got much longer here, and I need to make sure that things are ready for my successor.
GOD	[*silkily*] I thought you wanted to look at the land that I am giving to the Israelites?

[*Pause*]

It is time for you to go and look.

MOSES   [*pause*] We've come to the end of the road, then?

GOD   [*pause*] Yes.

MOSES   [*not quite believing*] This is it? My work is done?

GOD   [*pause*] Yes.

MOSES   [*mentally shaking himself*] Then I'd better get on with it, hadn't I?

[*Pause*]

But first let me appoint a new leader – someone who will guide the nation when I'm gone. Someone who will care for the people as I have cared for them. You know what they're like—

GOD   [*amused*] Yes – sheep!

MOSES   [*smiling*] And sheep without a leader get into trouble.

GOD   I rather thought they managed that *with* a leader.

MOSES   True.

GOD   What about Joshua, Nun's son? He'll make a good successor for you.

MOSES   [*grudgingly agreeing*] Joshua? Yes, he's not bad – could be suitable, if he had some help.

GOD   Could be suitable? He'll be great! As good as you've been.

MOSES   If you say so. But will the people obey him? They can be difficult to handle—

GOD   [*interrupting*] And you would know!

79

MOSES   [*ignoring the interruption*] —especially if they think I'm going to return.

GOD   Call the people together, make Joshua stand before the priest, Eleazar, and announce to the people that I, the Lord, have appointed him as your successor.

MOSES   That *might* work, especially if he's guided by Eleazar and by you in the early days.

GOD   [*confidently*] It *will* work.

       [*Pause*]

       Now, about this trip up to the top of Mount Abarim—

29
Joshua's first talk with God
Joshua 1

GOD   Joshua! It's time you and I had a talk. We need to get some things straight.

JOSHUA   [*startled*] What? Who's that? Is there somebody there?

GOD   Joshua! Are you listening?

       [*Pause*]

       [*Getting irritated*] Joshua!

JOSHUA   [*very nervous*] Who is it?

GOD   Who do you think it is? The abominable snowman? It's me!

JOSHUA   [*unsure*] God? Is that you, God?

GOD   Of course it is. Who else do you think it could be in the middle of the desert – where there's not a blade of grass or a tree, let alone another human being?

JOSHUA   [*shyly*] I wasn't sure. We've not spoken before, have we?

GOD   And whose fault's that?

JOSHUA   [*trying to explain*] I thought you only spoke to Moses.

GOD   [*shocked*] 'Only spoke to Moses'?

JOSHUA   Yes, isn't that right?

GOD   Well, I suppose I've certainly had more to do with Moses recently than anyone else, but I've been with many of your forefathers in the past – with Abraham, Isaac and with Joseph.

JOSHUA   [*awed*] And now with me?

GOD   And now with you. There's work to be done, it's time for my people to cross the River Jordan.

JOSHUA   [*nervously*] But that's going to be dangerous. The Canaanites have no love for us.

GOD   [*grandly, ignoring Joshua*] I am giving the whole of the land to my people, from the great deserts of the south to the mountains in the north; from the Jordan in the east to the Mediterranean Sea in the west. All of this land I am giving to you!

JOSHUA   [*dubiously cynical*] Thanks! I suppose the Canaanites are just going to hand it over to us, are they? 'Here you are Israel, have our land, it's all yours.'

GOD   [*icily*] There's no need to get cynical, Joshua, it doesn't suit a young man.

JOSHUA   Well, it's all right for you. We're the ones that must fight the battle. The Canaanites won't allow us just to walk into your Promised Land, will they?

GOD   No, it won't be easy! But I can promise you this – if you obey my words, no-one will be able to defeat you; and I will be with you, as I was with Moses.

JOSHUA   [*thinking*] You're asking rather a lot, aren't you? I've never led the people of Israel before. Who's to say that they will follow me?

GOD   Be determined and confident, and the people will follow you—

JOSHUA   [*interrupting*] You're *definitely* asking a lot!

GOD   [*still continuing*] —and obey the Law that Moses gave to you—

JOSHUA   In fact you're asking the *impossible*! How on earth am I supposed to carry out all these instructions. I can't do it!

GOD   [*continuing unabated*] —*and* keep determined and be confident. Don't become afraid! I will be with you always.

JOSHUA   [*pause*] Have you finished?

GOD   For the moment, why?

JOSHUA   Right! Now it's time for me to have my say.

GOD   If you say so.

JOSHUA   [*determined*] Well, I won't do it! You'll have to get someone else. I can't lead the people. I'm simply not capable of doing it. You need a superman to lead the people of Israel into Canaan.

GOD   [*positively*] No, I need you, Joshua. You will lead my people very well indeed.

JOSHUA   [*getting desperate*] I won't! I can't! I'm not cut out for it. After all Moses had enough trouble with the people, and I'm no Moses.

GOD   [*implacably*] No-one will be able to defeat you, and I *will* be with you always.

JOSHUA   [*beginning to listen*] Always?

GOD   Always.

JOSHUA   No-one will defeat us?

GOD   No-one.

JOSHUA   [*pause*] You always supported Moses, didn't you?

GOD   Yes.

JOSHUA   You never let him down.

GOD   He rarely let me down.

JOSHUA	[*pause*] All right, I'll give it a go. I guess all I can do is trust you?
GOD	That's all I'm asking of you – to trust me. That's all I've ever asked your forefathers.

30

Gideon's call

Judges 6.11–18

GOD	Gideon of Ophrah, I wish to speak to you!
GIDEON	Who are you?
GOD	It's no matter, for the moment. You are Gideon of Ophrah, son of Joash, are you not?
GIDEON	What if I am? What's it to you?
GOD	I wish to talk to you.
GIDEON	I'm busy, as you can see!
GOD	Threshing wheat?
GIDEON	[*urgently*] Ssh! If the Midianites hear you, there'll be trouble.
GOD	[*surprised*] Threshing wheat, in a wine press?
GIDEON	It's the only way to keep it secret, the only way to preserve what we have from the raiders.
GOD	Come here, and listen to me for a moment! You can surely leave what you are doing for a moment?
GIDEON	Very well, but it had better be worthwhile. We cannot afford to lose this wheat to the Midianites.
GOD	Oh, my words are surely worthwhile!
GIDEON	Wait a second and I'll cover the winepress from sight.

GOD You are a brave and strong man, Gideon.

GIDEON [*laughing*] I don't know about that. It makes sense to do what I can for the family. It's little enough.

GOD No, I don't mean that!

GIDEON [*puzzled*] No?

GOD The Lord is with you, Gideon.

GIDEON H'm! If the Lord is with me, I'm not Gideon.

GOD What do you mean?

GIDEON If the Lord is with me, why has all this happened to us?

GOD All what?

GIDEON The Midianites! The way they have attacked us and oppressed us recently. How can you say 'the Lord is with me'?

GOD [*ironically*] I can surely say that he is.

GIDEON Well, it's all right for you to say he's with us. But in the past God used to do such marvellous things.

GOD Such as?

GIDEON What about the way that he saved our people.

GOD When?

GIDEON When he brought them out of Egypt, and rescued us from Pharaoh?

GOD Oh, then!

GIDEON [*irritated*] Yes, then! And guided them through the desert, giving them food and drink—

GOD [*to himself*] Among other things!

GIDEON But now the Lord has left us.

GOD He hasn't.

GIDEON He's abandoned us into the hands of the Midianites.

GOD You think so?

GIDEON I know so. The Midianites have ravaged our land and killed our people.

GOD Then go and rescue Israel from the Midianites.

GIDEON [*to himself*] 'Go and rescue Israel', he says.

[*Laughing*]

You must be joking. Just how am I supposed to do that? My clan is the smallest in the tribe of Manasseh, and I am one of the least of my family.

GOD   Nevertheless, go and do as I say.

GIDEON   And who are you to say 'Go and rescue Israel'?

GOD   I am God, the God of Israel.

GIDEON   [*laughing*] God! That's a good one! And I'm God's assistant!

GOD   Well, that's true as well.

GIDEON   [*pause*] Who did you say you were?

GOD   God.

GIDEON   The God of Abraham, Isaac and Jacob?

GOD   Yes, also the God of Gideon and the people of Israel.

GIDEON   Gosh!

[*Pause*]

And you think I could rescue Israel from the hordes of Midian?

GOD   Yes, with my help you will crush the Midianites as though they were only one man.

GIDEON   Forgive me, God, but would you give me a sign?

GOD   Of what?

GIDEON   A sign that you are who you say you are.

GOD   And when I have given you a sign?

GIDEON   I will carry out your work in clearing this land of the Midianites.

GOD   [*laughing*] As I said, you are a brave and strong man, Gideon. I will give you a sign.

31

Advance news of Samson

Judges 13

MANOAH   God, have you a moment?

GOD   [*grandly*] Yes, Manoah, I have as many moments as you wish.

MANOAH   Well, that's good.

GOD   Why?

MANOAH   It may take some time.

GOD   That sounds ominous.

MANOAH   [*amused*] No, it's nothing like that. I just want to ask some questions, that's all.

GOD   Right.
[*Pause*]
Well? Go ahead, then. I'm waiting.

MANOAH   [*gulps nervously*] You are?

GOD   [*uncompromisingly*] Yes.

MANOAH   That's not so easy.

GOD   What's the matter? I'm listening.
[*Laughs at own joke*]
I'm all ears, as it were!

MANOAH   Well, I don't know quite how to put this.

GOD   [*baldly*] Just say it.

MANOAH   Oh, all right. Here goes.
[*Pause, then in a rush*]
Did you send *someone* to Zorah, yesterday?

GOD   [*thinking*] Zorah?
[*Pause, then meditatively*]
Zorah.

MANOAH   Yes, you know. The town where I live?

GOD	Oh, that Zorah!
MANOAH	Well, where did you think I meant?
GOD	I was only teasing you. Zorah in Palestine – yes, I know it.
MANOAH	Well, did you?
GOD	Did I what?
MANOAH	[*irritated*] *Did* you send anyone to visit Zorah?
GOD	Like who?
MANOAH	Well, I don't know what to call him – an emissary, a messenger, a—
GOD	[*calmly, interrupting*] You mean, an *angel*?
MANOAH	[*trying to be blasé*] Er, yes, an angel. Exactly!
GOD	I *did* send an angel to Zorah.
MANOAH	You did? Oh, that's all right, then.
GOD	It is?
MANOAH	Yes.
GOD	But you wanted to know something else?
MANOAH	I did, if you don't mind.
GOD	I don't mind at all. What do you want to know?
MANOAH	Your messenger, or rather, the angel you sent—
GOD	Yes?
MANOAH	He said that we would have a son.
GOD	Yes?
MANOAH	*Yes?* [*Amazed*] You mean it's *true*?
GOD	It's true.
MANOAH	I can't believe it! We've waited so long to have children that I thought we'd never have a son. It seems too good to be true!
GOD	You didn't believe my messenger, then?
MANOAH	[*ashamed*] I'm sorry, but you see I needed to be certain. I wondered if my wife might have dreamt it.

GOD   Oh, it's quite certain. Your wife will definitely have a son.

MANOAH   I don't know whether to laugh or cry. We've been so desperate to have children.

GOD   I know.

MANOAH   We'd given up, thinking it was too late.

GOD   I know that.

MANOAH   And not only are we to have a son, but the angel said he is to be a Nazirite?

GOD   Yes, you are to make sure that he drinks no strong drink, nor cuts his hair.

MANOAH   But, Lord, we need to know more than that about the way he is to be brought up.

GOD   What do you need to know?

MANOAH   The life of a Nazirite is so difficult. How is he to live? What work must he do as he grows up?

GOD   Your son will be dedicated to me—

MANOAH   [interrupting] In what way? How do you mean?

GOD   He will start the work of removing the Philistines from your country—

MANOAH   [interrupting] We're going to be free? They've been our masters for so long.

GOD   Remember, your job is to bring up this child. You are to teach him my ways, and prepare him for the work he has to do.

MANOAH   What shall we call him, Lord? What is to be his name?

GOD   His name is to be Samson, and he will have strength denied to other people.

MANOAH   Samson. That is a good, strong name.

GOD   Remember you are to teach him about me, for he is to be my servant.

MANOAH   [*picking up the theme*] And he is to free your people from the Philistines.

GOD   Exactly.

32

Who's there?

1 Samuel 3.1–13

GOD   Samuel!
[*Pause*]
Samuel!
[*Pause, then calls again, getting a little irritated this time*]
Samuel!

SAMUEL   [*half asleep*] Yes, Eli! I'm just coming!

GOD   [*as if to himself*] Well that's a fib, if ever I heard one. You're still snuggled down under your blanket. It's always the same with teenagers, call and call them, but you only get 'I'm coming!'

SAMUEL   [*huffily talking to himself*] Well, how would you like it? You'd moan if I came and shouted at you just as you were going off to sleep.

GOD   Shouted at you? That's certainly fib number two! I only whispered at you.

SAMUEL   [*getting quite sulky now*] Well, it's so quiet here in the Temple your voice *sounded* loud.
[*Pause*]
Well if there's nothing else, I'm going back to sleep. I'll

89

	soon have to get up to tend the lamps, and if I don't manage to get some sleep now I'll be lucky to get any before you have me on the go again tomorrow.
GOD	Heh! Wait a minute!
SAMUEL	[*just remembering what has been said*] And what do you mean, 'It's always the same with teenagers'? I've worked hard all week, keeping things clean, helping with the visitors, lighting the lamps, and if that isn't enough you expect me to do my studies as well.
GOD	[*slightly amused*] Sorry, Samuel! I didn't mean to upset you.
SAMUEL	Good!
	[*Pause*]
	Was there anything else you wanted?
GOD	Oh, yes! I have a message for you, about Eli.
SAMUEL	[*long pause*] About *Eli*?
	[*Pause*]
	Then *who* are you? I thought you were Eli? And how come you managed to get into the Temple at this time of night? How did you get past the guards? You'd better get out again quickly before Eli finds out. You're not supposed to be here, you know!
GOD	[*amused*] Aren't I? I rather thought I was.
SAMUEL	No! No! Eli's most insistent that the people don't enter here. This is God's special place, he says.
GOD	I know.
SAMUEL	So you'd better leave quickly. I'll see what I can do to find a way out for you, without anyone knowing.
GOD	Very kind of you, Samuel. But I think I rather like it here.
SAMUEL	[*agitated*] No! No! You must leave!
	[*A sudden thought occurs to him*]
	Who are you, anyway?

GOD   Jehovah, Yahweh, God, I am who I am – you may take
               your pick of the names.

SAMUEL   [*shocked*] Stop! Stop! That's blasphemous! You can't
               say things like that. Our God strikes people dead for
               less than that. He's a jealous God, and he doesn't like
               his name being taken in vain. Please, please, stop!

GOD   [*amused*] It's all right, Samuel, don't panic! I *am* God.
               It's me talking to you.

SAMUEL   [*still shocked*] Oh, but that's even worse. Please don't
               talk in this way, you don't know what you're doing!
               [*Loudly, as though to God*]
               It's all right, God. He doesn't know what he's saying.
               Please don't get angry with him.

GOD   [*patiently explaining, as if to someone a little slow*]
               Samuel, I *am* God. I'm hardly going to get cross with
               myself, am I?

SAMUEL   [*beginning to listen*] You're God?
               [*Still not quite sure*]
               Talking to *me*?

GOD   Yes, talking to *you*.

SAMUEL   I don't believe it!

GOD   [*getting a little fed up*] Don't tell me I've got to go
               through that again!

SAMUEL   Through what again?

GOD   [*parodying a conversation*] 'How do I know you're
               really God? Give me some proof that you are who
               you say you are.'

SAMUEL   Oh, I see what you mean. Does everyone say that to
               you? It must get a bit boring if no-one ever believes you.

GOD   [*succinctly*] It does.

SAMUEL   [*taking a decision*] OK, I won't ask for proof, though
               it's asking a bit much to expect me to swallow it hook,
               line and sinker first time, isn't it?

GOD   [*laughing*] I suppose it is, Samuel. But you will.
SAMUEL   I will.
          [*As though saying a creed*]
          You are God, Jehovah, Yahweh, the God of my Fathers.
          OK, speak, Lord. Your servant is listening.

33

Israel wants a king

1 Samuel 8

SAMUEL   God, there's a slight problem.
GOD   Only a *slight* problem? Well, that's good. It's usually a
          large problem.
SAMUEL   Well, I say a *slight problem*, but you might not like it.
GOD   [*ironically*] Really! You do amaze me!
SAMUEL   You see, it's the people.
GOD   It usually is. It's rarely you, is it?
SAMUEL   Well, I am their spokesman, aren't I?
GOD   True.
SAMUEL   And as their spokesman, they've sent me to ask you a
          question.
GOD   Go on.
SAMUEL   [*embarrassed*] It's about my sons.
GOD   Joel and Abijah?
SAMUEL   Yes.
GOD   [*sternly*] You made them judges in Beersheba, as I
          remember?
SAMUEL   Yes.

GOD	Well, it was *your* decision.
SAMUEL	[*sighs*] I know. Not one of my better decisions, though.
GOD	Definitely not, I'd say.
SAMUEL	They've not proved a success.
GOD	More than that, they're only interested in making money.
SAMUEL	I know.
GOD	They've accepted bribes, and not judged cases honestly.
SAMUEL	I know.
GOD	So what's new?
SAMUEL	It's the people. They're not happy.
GOD	I'm not surprised, are you?
SAMUEL	The leaders came to speak to me, when I was in Ramah.
GOD	And what did they want?
SAMUEL	I'm getting old.
GOD	Aren't we all?
SAMUEL	They're worried what will happen when I die.
GOD	Justifiably by the sound of it.
SAMUEL	They imagine there might be trouble from Joel and Abijah.
GOD	And they're probably right.
SAMUEL	So, well, this is the awkward bit—
GOD	[*interrupting*] Go on! Spit it out!
SAMUEL	[*in a rush*] They want me to appoint a king to rule over them.
GOD	A *king*?
SAMUEL	Yes, a king. They want to be like the other countries round about us, and have their own king.
GOD	What do you think?
SAMUEL	[*sadly*] They don't want me.
GOD	No, it's not you they don't want. They are rejecting *me* as their king.
SAMUEL	You?

93

GOD   [*angrily*] Ever since I brought them out of Egypt they have turned away from me. They have ignored my wishes, and they have worshipped other gods. Now they are doing to you what they have done to me.

SAMUEL   But what am I to say to them?

GOD   Give in to them.

SAMUEL   *What*?

GOD   Tell them they can have a king.

SAMUEL   Really?

GOD   Yes, then warn them what will happen.

SAMUEL   What do you mean?

GOD   A king will take their sons as soldiers for his army. A king will make their sons plough his fields before their own.

SAMUEL   I bet they hadn't thought of that.

GOD   A king will take their daughters to work in his kitchen.

SAMUEL   They won't like that.

GOD   A king will take the best fields, the best vineyards, and he will demand a tenth of their corn and olive oil.

SAMUEL   They *definitely* won't like that.

GOD   And lastly, he will make slaves of them.

SAMUEL   [*horrified*] No!

GOD   Yes, and when that happens—

SAMUEL   Yes?

GOD   —it will be no good them complaining to me.

SAMUEL   [*understanding*] Because they have chosen to have a king.

GOD   Exactly. They have chosen their own damnation. It will be no good appealing to me, then.

SAMUEL   I will go and tell them all this, my Lord God.

GOD   [*sadly*] But they will not listen, Samuel. They will not listen to you.

34

Samuel finds a king

1 Samuel 9–10

GOD   Samuel?

SAMUEL   Yes, Lord?

GOD   Have you seen him yet?

SAMUEL   Who, Lord?

GOD   [*exasperated*] Give me patience! Who did I send you out to see, yesterday?

SAMUEL   [*light dawning*] Oh, sorry! You mean, the man called Saul.

GOD   Yes, of course I do.

SAMUEL   Well I've been a little busy since then, what with one thing and another.

GOD   Samuel! *Did you find him?*

SAMUEL   [*casually*] Yes. I saw Saul this morning. He came asking for the Seer, to see if I could find some missing donkeys for him.

GOD   Yes?

SAMUEL   [*getting side-tracked*] I seem to have become a Lost Property Bureau recently! People do come to ask me the most amazing things. You know the other day someone actually came to ask whether or not—

GOD   [*interrupting*] Perhaps you should take up a new profession.

SAMUEL   [*amused*] It might make more money.

GOD   I doubt it! Now, about Saul.

SAMUEL   Amazing man, isn't he?

GOD   What?

SAMUEL   Saul – his height. I've never seen a man so tall before.

GOD	Ah, yes, amazing!
SAMUEL	And pretty handsome. All the women were after him, I noticed.
GOD	Yes, they would be. By the way, what did you do with him?
SAMUEL	I sent him to my home for some food. He and his servant had been on the road for some days, by the sound of it. They looked in need of a good meal and a bath.
GOD	That's good.
SAMUEL	By the way, why did you want me to find this young man?
GOD	[*bald statement*] He is to become king of Israel.
SAMUEL	[*amazed*] What?
GOD	He is to be king.
SAMUEL	Really? I don't believe it.
GOD	Why not?
SAMUEL	[*amazed*] Well, a member of the tribe of Benjamin?
GOD	What's wrong with that?
SAMUEL	But *Benjamin*? It's the smallest of all the tribes! What good has ever come from Benjamin, I ask you?
GOD	A king for Israel?
SAMUEL	But *Benjamin*!
GOD	Anyway, it is the tribe I have chosen.
SAMUEL	Who's his father? What family does he come from? What's his ancestry? Surely there must be something we can say of him.
GOD	He's the son of Kish.
SAMUEL	Kish? Isn't he very wealthy? I seem to have heard so.
GOD	Yes.
SAMUEL	[*sigh*] Well, that's something in his favour.
GOD	[*ironically*] I'm so glad you think there's something in his favour, Samuel.

SAMUEL	Well it's all a bit odd, but if he's your chosen man, OK! What do you want me to do, God?
GOD	Tomorrow morning, when Saul leaves your house, you are to anoint him.
SAMUEL	Anoint him? What with?
GOD	Take a jar of olive oil and pour it onto Saul's head, as a symbol of the office for which I have chosen him—
SAMUEL	[*interrupting*] Do I tell him what is to happen to him? Does he know already?
GOD	[*continuing as though uninterrupted*] —Then you are to tell him that from this day onwards I, his God, have *chosen* him.
SAMUEL	But shall I tell him what he has been chosen *for*?
GOD	Yes. He is being anointed as king of Israel.
SAMUEL	I shall do as you say.
GOD	And you are to command him to protect my people, for from now onwards they are to be his people. He is to be their ruler.
SAMUEL	When is he to be proclaimed king to the people?
GOD	Also tell him not to be afraid for I will be with him from now on, and I will guide him.
SAMUEL	Yes, but when will the people be told?
GOD	When the time is ready he will be acclaimed king by all the people. It is enough for now that he is to be the anointed one.

35

Samuel anoints another king

1 Samuel 15–16

GOD	Samuel! I am *really* displeased with you!
SAMUEL	[*surprised*] You are, God? Why? What on earth have I done?
GOD	I've been trying to contact you for the past few weeks, and I never get a reply. What is the matter?
SAMUEL	Nothing, Lord, nothing.
GOD	Well, why haven't I heard from you?
SAMUEL	I didn't know you wanted me.
GOD	[*crossly*] You didn't *know* I wanted you?
SAMUEL	I was rather busy.
GOD	I thought you were supposed to be my man in Israel.
SAMUEL	I am.
GOD	Well, it would be rather helpful if my *man in Israel* kept in contact with headquarters.
SAMUEL	[*to himself*] Not from my point of view.
GOD	What was that Samuel? You've taken to muttering.
SAMUEL	Have I?
GOD	*And* you've taken to avoiding me, haven't you?
SAMUEL	Only because I know what you want to talk about.
GOD	Which is?
SAMUEL	King Saul.
GOD	Well there you're wrong, for once.
SAMUEL	[*astonished*] You don't want to talk about King Saul?
GOD	No, for there's no such person—
SAMUEL	[*interrupting*] As King Saul?
GOD	King Saul does not exist any more, as you well know.
SAMUEL	Yes, he does. He still lives in Gibeah.

GOD   But he is not king of Israel.

SAMUEL I know, because *you* rejected him.

GOD   Because *he* disobeyed my commands.

SAMUEL But I'm sorry for him.

GOD   Oh, Samuel! How long will you grieve for him? I have rejected him as king of Israel. It's time to choose another king for the people.

SAMUEL [*to himself*] I knew I should have ignored him.

GOD   What was that, Samuel?

SAMUEL Nothing, Lord, nothing.

GOD   Good. It's time to take your olive oil for anointing, and go to Bethlehem.

SAMUEL [*grumbling to himself*] Bethlehem? What good has ever come out of Bethlehem?

GOD   Are you still complaining?

SAMUEL Not at all, Lord! Bethlehem, you said. And where shall I go when I get there?

GOD   You are to find a man named Jesse.

SAMUEL [*horrified*] Hang on a moment! I can't go to *Bethlehem*.

GOD   Why ever not?

SAMUEL Do you think I'm tired of living?

GOD   [*wearily*] I sometimes think you must be.

SAMUEL Ha! Ha! I'm not talking about you, God. I'm talking about *Saul*.

GOD   What about Saul?

SAMUEL If he hears I've gone to Bethlehem to anoint someone else as king he will have me killed, that's for sure.

GOD   A good point.

SAMUEL So what on earth do I do?

GOD   Go to Bethlehem—

SAMUEL [*interrupting*] You've said that once, and I've just told you what will happen.

GOD   [*icily*] If you'd let me finish!

SAMUEL   [*humbly*] Sorry.

GOD   Go to Bethlehem. Take a calf with you, and let everyone know that you've come to offer a sacrifice.

SAMUEL   [*doubtfully*] Yes, what then? This doesn't sound a very good plan to me.

GOD   *Then* invite Jesse to the sacrifice.

SAMUEL   But who is the person to be anointed king?

GOD   I will tell you who to anoint, if you'd just stop talking for a moment! He is one of Jesse's sons.

SAMUEL   [*jumping in again*] The eldest son, I suppose.

GOD   Did I choose the eldest son, last time?

SAMUEL   No, you didn't.

GOD   I do not choose in the way that you, or any man, would choose.

SAMUEL   Then how do you choose?

GOD   I do not judge a person by their looks. I judge by what I see in their heart.

SAMUEL   And who—

GOD   I have chosen David, the *youngest* son of Jesse, to be the next king of Israel. He is to be my anointed king, and in due course he will be proclaimed king of Israel by all the people.

36

David and the Philistines

2 Samuel 5.6–25

DAVID   Well, I've done it, at last.

GOD   What's that?

DAVID   [*overjoyed*] I've done it! I've actually done it!

GOD   Done what?

DAVID   I'm now the king.

GOD   Really.

DAVID   [*gloating*] I'm the king of the *whole of Israel*!

GOD   *You've* done it, you say?

DAVID   Oh, you know what I mean, *we've* done it. I'm now king of Judah *and* Israel.

GOD   *And* Jerusalem.

DAVID   [*laughing*] Jerusalem too! The Jebusites thought I couldn't overcome them. They thought their strong walls would save them. They hid behind the walls of Jerusalem, jeering at me. At me! At King David!

GOD   [*ironically*] Pity they forgot about the water tunnel.

DAVID   It was a little wet, but it served the purpose. It took us right into the heart of the city.

GOD   Don't forget to have it blocked up! You don't want your enemies using it against you in the future.

DAVID   I hear that even Hiram, king of Tyre, has sent emissaries to ask for peace. I knew I could do it!

GOD   [*coughing*]

DAVID   Sorry, *we* could do it.

GOD   That's better.

DAVID   [*solemnly*] But—

GOD   But?

DAVID   *But* I now have a rather big problem.

GOD   You have?

DAVID   Yes.

GOD   What's wrong? I thought you'd got everything you wanted.

DAVID   I do.

GOD   So?

DAVID   So, the Philistines have heard that I've taken Jerusalem.

GOD   [*pause*] And what's wrong with that?

DAVID   [*animated*] What's wrong with that? Are you mad?

GOD   [*mildly ironic*] I don't think so. An interesting question: is God mad?

DAVID   Oh, you know what I mean. Forgive me, Lord.

GOD   [*still mild*] Sometimes, David, you go too far.

DAVID   Sorry, it's just I got carried away, thinking about the Philistines.

GOD   OK, apology accepted. Now tell me all about them.

DAVID   Although we've only just captured Jerusalem, we're going to have to get out of the city if we're to survive.

GOD   This sounds a bit drastic.

DAVID   It *will* be drastic if we don't leave now.

GOD   Really?

DAVID   There won't be any pieces to pick up if I don't move quickly.

GOD   Very drastic! Where are you thinking of going?

DAVID   Somewhere quiet. Somewhere safe. Somewhere away from the Philistines.

GOD   Like where?

DAVID   I don't know where. I'll have to think about it.

GOD   [*mildly*] Of course you could stay and fight.

DAVID   [*horrified*] You must be joking! Do you think I want to end my life just as it's starting to get interesting? No, I'll leave Jerusalem tomorrow morning.

GOD   Please yourself, it's your life after all. It was only a *suggestion*.

DAVID   What was?

GOD   Fighting the Philistines.

DAVID   Have you any idea how fierce they are?
[*Realising to whom he is talking*]
Well, of course you do.

GOD   They're sea people, more accustomed to fighting at sea, or near the sea. Here, well, *here* they're, well, *inland*.

DAVID   That's true.

GOD   You're a seasoned fighter, and you know about *land* fighting.

DAVID   True.

GOD   So where would be a good place to ambush the Philistines?

DAVID   [*definitely*] A valley! Somewhere like Rephaim, perhaps.

GOD   There you are! Lure them to Rephaim.

DAVID   It might work.

GOD   [*cheerfully*] Of course it will work. After all you have a secret weapon.

DAVID   [*surprised*] I do?

GOD   You *do*.

DAVID   What secret weapon do I have that the Philistines don't have?

GOD   You and all the people of Israel have *God* on your side.

DAVID   You will help us defeat them?

GOD   Go, David! I *will* help you defeat the Philistines. I, the Lord your God, have spoken.

37

David chooses a successor

1 Kings 1

DAVID   Lord, God! Are you listening?
       [*Pause*]
       I know it's been some time since we spoke—
       [*Pause*]
       Are you there? It's David, I need your help.

GOD   [*sternly*] I am here.

DAVID   [*relieved*] I thought you'd deserted me. Everyone else seems to have left, except Abishag the Shunamite girl.

GOD   Seems to me you're surrounded by dozens of people.

DAVID   They don't really care about me.

GOD   Abishag seems to care for you.

DAVID   Yes, she has looked after me well in my old age.

GOD   Your servants too.

DAVID   True, but as for everyone else they are just waiting for me to die.

GOD   You think so?

DAVID   I *know so*!

GOD   Why do you think that is?

DAVID   It's a question of who should become king, you see.

GOD   I might have guessed! It's always a question of who will be the next king.

DAVID   Which son should inherit after me?

GOD   *After* you?

DAVID   Well, you've got me there!

GOD   [*puzzled*] Yes?

DAVID   Yes, I gather Adonijah's got there ahead of time!

GOD   You don't say?

DAVID	*[angrily]* I do! He's invited all his brothers, and a number of leaders in Judah to join him at the Stone of Zoheleth, to make a sacrifice.
GOD	So I heard.
DAVID	In other words, he's already proclaimed himself king!
GOD	But *you* are the king of Israel, David.
DAVID	I *am* glad to hear you say that. I'd begun to wonder if there was something I didn't know.
GOD	Like what?
DAVID	That perhaps you'd withdrawn your support from me.
GOD	David, don't you know me better than that? I would have told you if that were the case.
DAVID	Well, thanks for that assurance. *[Rather nervously]* I know I've let you down during my life.
GOD	*[solemnly]* You have, David. But at the moment you still have my support. I chose you and made you king over my people.
DAVID	But perhaps it's time we looked at my successor, Lord?
GOD	*I have looked!* *[Pause]* What are *your* conclusions?
DAVID	There are two obvious choices. Should it be Haggith's son, Adonijah, or should it be Bathsheba's son, Solomon?
GOD	So? Your conclusions?
DAVID	Nathan.
GOD	*[puzzled]* The prophet?
DAVID	Yes.
GOD	*[enlightened]* Ah, yes! What does Nathan say?
DAVID	It was he who came to tell me that Adonijah had proclaimed himself king. He's furious.
GOD	*[smiling]* He would be.

DAVID   [*wryly*] Nathan wasn't invited to the sacrifice, neither was Zadok the priest.

GOD   Very ominous.

DAVID   Nathan wanted to know why he hadn't been told that *I'd* proclaimed Adonijah to be my successor.

GOD   [*wryly*] Sounds as though he thinks you're dead already.

DAVID   [*continuing*] *Then* I had Bathsheba on the doorstep!

GOD   Metaphorically speaking, of course.

DAVID   Yes, she actually invaded my *bedchamber*!

GOD   To remind you that you'd promised the crown to her son, Solomon?

DAVID   Exactly!

GOD   A formidable woman, Bathsheba.

DAVID   [*with feeling*] Definitely!

GOD   And what did you say?

DAVID   What I hoped you'd agree with.

GOD   Which was?

DAVID   I agreed to nominate Solomon as the next king.

GOD   And?

DAVID   Sent him down with Nathan to Gihon where he is to be anointed with oil, as the future king of Israel.

GOD   Well done, David. You have done *very well indeed*! Solomon will be the next king of Israel.

38

The man who spoke against Bethel

1 Kings 13

GOD   Man of God, are you listening?

MAN   [*worried*] Who is it who speaks to me?

GOD   It is your God who speaks.

MAN   [*scared*] Lord, God? Really?

GOD   [*amused*] Really.

MAN   [*very worried*] What have I done wrong that you wish to speak to me?

GOD   Don't be so worried, man of God. You have been faithful to me.

MAN   [*still nervous*] Well, I have always tried to follow your laws, as best I can.

GOD   You have.

MAN   [*plucking up courage*] So what do you want?

GOD   I have a job for you to do.

MAN   [*worried again*] Don't ask me to *do* something, God. I'm not exactly your man of action. You must know that.

GOD   Do you need to be a fighter to work for me?

MAN   And to be honest, those who work for you don't seem to live very long, do they?

GOD   Well that's telling me, I suppose.

MAN   I've always been honest with you, haven't I?

GOD   True.

              [*Pause*]

              Who do you fear most, man of God – me or other men?

MAN   [*pause*] All right! You've got me! I suppose I have to fear you most.

GOD   So you'll do what I want, then?

MAN   [*reluctantly*] Yes, if I *must*, I suppose I will.

GOD   [*sternly*] You *must*!

MAN   [*sighing*] So what do I have to do, then?

GOD   You are to go to Bethel.

MAN   And when I get to Bethel?

GOD   You are to speak out against the altar there—

MAN   [*horrified*] You *must* be joking. I won't last a moment if I do that. They'll *all* be after my blood!

GOD   [*continuing*] Then, you are to warn the people that in future the priests themselves will be sacrificed on the altar.

MAN   [*horrified*] What?

GOD   When one of David's family has a son called Josiah, the priests worshipping at Bethel will not be *my* priests.

MAN   [*grumbling*] Well, I suppose that's something. I thought for a moment you were saying that the priests who worship there now were to be sacrificed on the altar.

GOD   *And* you are to give the people a sign. The altar will break apart and the ashes on it will fall to the ground when you proclaim these words.

MAN   [*ironically*] I should think *I'll* fall to the ground, permanently, if I say that!

GOD   Don't be so hen-hearted!

MAN   [*to himself*] *Hen-hearted* he says! H'm! It's all right for him, he hasn't got to *go* to Bethel.

GOD   And while you are there, King Jeroboam will hear your words.

MAN   [*appalled*] King Jeroboam!
[*Determined*]
Oh, no, that's it, I'm not going! He and King Rehoboam are at logger-heads. I'm not getting caught up in their private war.

GOD   [*sternly*] Man of God, will you listen to me?

MAN   No thanks! I'm off!

GOD   Man of God, if you will obey me, you will not be in danger.

MAN   [*hesitating*] Truly?

GOD   Truly, man of God. You have my word.

MAN   I will be *safe*?

GOD   *If* you obey my words, all will be well. But you must not return by the same road that you take to Bethel.

MAN   Oh, that's no problem, I can take another way back to Judah.

GOD   Neither are you to eat or drink while you are at Bethel.

MAN   Well, that's a little harder.

[*Pause*]

I like my food.

[*Doubtfully*]

However, I suppose I *could* do as you ask.

GOD   While you are carrying out this task, I will protect you from all danger.

MAN   Then I hope I don't meet King Jeroboam, because I'll certainly need your help if I do.

GOD   Have no fear. If you—

MAN   [*interrupting*] I know. If I obey your commands, I will be safe.

GOD   [*sternly*] Then heed my words, and obey them, man of God.

39

The prophet gives a warning
1 Kings 14

GOD	Ahijah, we need to talk urgently.
AHIJAH	What?
GOD	My prophet, we need to talk.
AHIJAH	We do?
GOD	We *do*!
AHIJAH	OK, I'm with you. What is it, God?
GOD	You're going to get a visitor very soon.
AHIJAH	A visitor?
	[*Laughs*]
	I get hundreds of visitors at Shiloh. Which one did you have in mind?
GOD	[*sarcastically*] Thank you, Ahijah, very helpful.
AHIJAH	[*still laughing*] Sorry, I couldn't resist it, God.
GOD	Your visitor is to be Jeroboam's wife.
AHIJAH	[*shocked*] What? *King* Jeroboam's wife?
GOD	Yes.
AHIJAH	Woah! Hang on! I don't like the sound of this much. I'm not going to get involved with King Jeroboam, it's too dangerous.
GOD	What you also need to know is that Jeroboam's wife will come in disguise.
AHIJAH	Oh, great! How am I supposed to know who she is? What am I talking about? I don't *want* to know who she is!
GOD	[*continuing*] You will know her, nevertheless. She will come to the shrine bringing with her ten loaves of bread, some cakes, and a jar of honey.

AHIJAH   [*sarcastically*] Very helpful! Half the women who come to Shiloh bring bread, cakes and honey.

GOD   [*ignoring him*] She will *also* ask about her son.

AHIJAH   [*not impressed*] And the *other half* ask about their sons.

GOD   You will know when she appears before you.

AHIJAH   [*even less impressed*] Have you forgotten that I'm an old man, and I'm blind?

GOD   No, Ahijah, I haven't forgotten you're blind. I will warn you when she arrives.

AHIJAH   Well, I can't say I'm very happy about it, but I suppose I've no choice. By the way, why is she coming?

GOD   She's coming to ask about her son, Abijah, who is ill.

AHIJAH   In other words she wants to know if he will live?

GOD   Yes, but I have a message for Jeroboam, that I wish you to give her.

AHIJAH   Oh, come on, Lord, have a heart. I daren't give him a message.

GOD   Ahijah, will you stop muttering and listen to me for a moment?

AHIJAH   Oh, go on! What am I supposed to tell him?

GOD   You are to give him some bad news.

AHIJAH   [*aghast*] Bad news!

GOD   Tell him that I chose him from among all the people of Israel to be king of Israel.

AHIJAH   Well, that's obvious! He must already know that.

GOD   [*continuing*] I took the kingdom away from David's family and gave it to him. But he has disobeyed my commands, unlike David, who was loyal to me.

AHIJAH   [*to himself*] I can't say I like the sound of this one bit.

GOD   He has rejected me, built idols and worshipped other gods.

AHIJAH   [*still to himself*] I *definitely* don't like the sound of this!

111

GOD	Because of this I will destroy him and his family. They will be swept away.
AHIJAH	[*appalled*] Oh, God!
GOD	Yes?
AHIJAH	Must I give the queen this message?
GOD	Yes, you must. You are also to tell her that I will punish Israel, and I will bring in a king who will put an end to Jeroboam's dynasty.
AHIJAH	[*resigned*] Well, I trust you will stay with me, and keep me safe, then. For there's no way I shall survive if I have to give this message. Jeroboam will sweep me away with one flick of his wrist – or rather, one swipe of his guard's sword!
GOD	Ahijah, obey me, and I will protect you from the king. For I am with you always.
AHIJAH	So be it, God. I will do as you command. And may you be with me always.

40

Elijah's first instructions

1 Kings 17

GOD	Elijah, are you going to answer me?
ELIJAH	Who's speaking?
GOD	Did you not hear me calling you before?
ELIJAH	I heard someone. Was it you?
GOD	[*amused*] Well, it wasn't the man in the moon!
ELIJAH	Who are you?

God	Who do you think?
Elijah	At a guess—
	[*Pause*]
	I don't know!
God	[*patiently*] That's no answer. Try again.
Elijah	You wouldn't by any chance be, no, it's not possible. I must be going out of my mind.
God	Neither is that any answer.
Elijah	Are you—
God	What?
Elijah	[*gulping*] God?
God	Of course.
Elijah	[*amazed*] Really?
God	Really.
Elijah	What on earth do you want with me?
God	I want you to work for me.
Elijah	Work for you? I don't know that I've got any talents.
God	Oh, you have, Elijah. You've got just what I want.
Elijah	I do?
God	Yes.
Elijah	What's the job?
God	You're going to be a prophet.
Elijah	[*amazed*] I am?
God	Yes. A *great* prophet.
Elijah	Wow!
	[*Pause*]
	And what would I have to do, as a prophet?
God	You will take messages to my people.
Elijah	A kind of go-between, then?
God	That's right.
Elijah	When do I start?
God	Today.
Elijah	Now?

GOD   Yes.

ELIJAH What is it? What message am I to take, and who is it for?

GOD   I want you to leave Gilead and go to King Ahab.

ELIJAH [*eagerly*] And when I get there, what then?

GOD   [*frowning*] If you'll wait a moment, I'll tell you.

ELIJAH Sorry, it's just so exciting.

GOD   *When* you get to the king you are to give him a message from me.

ELIJAH What's the message?

GOD   Tell him that he has sinned against me, by worshipping Baal, by building temples to him, and by making an image of the goddess Asherah. Because of this there will be no rain for the next three years in his country, and I will cause a drought to come upon all the land.

ELIJAH He's going to *love that*!

GOD   More to the point he's not going to *love you*, or me, for that matter.

ELIJAH In other words I'd better get out of the area pretty fast after I've given him the message.

GOD   Get ready to leave immediately, and find somewhere safe to stay for a while.

ELIJAH [*thinking*] What about that place I went to some years ago.

GOD   Which one was that?

ELIJAH Across the Jordan, to the east. I can't remember the name—

GOD   I know! That place near the River Cherith! Yes, it's very isolated, the king will never think of looking for you there.

ELIJAH [*with feeling*] I sincerely hope not. I don't think I want to know what he'll do to me if he finds me.

GOD   [*still planning*] The river will give you water to drink.

114

ELIJAH But what do I do for food? It's almost complete desert there.

GOD I'll send some bread and meat to you every morning and evening.

ELIJAH [*sarcastically*] Oh? And how will you get it to such an isolated place? By pigeon carrier-post?

GOD [*matter-of-factly*] No, raven-post!

ELIJAH [*to himself*] By *raven* he says! Next he'll be sending it by *wolf*.

GOD [*irritated*] I said *by raven* and I meant *by raven*. Trust me, Elijah, and all will be well.

ELIJAH It's not your skin that's up-for-grabs, God. It's mine!

GOD [*to himself*] One of these days there will be a prophet who just trusts me. I look forward immensely to that day.

ELIJAH [*put out*] Well, it doesn't help to have one's God saying he's going to send food to you by a *raven*, does it? It *sounds* like a joke, not something that will actually happen.

GOD [*amused*] That's true, I suppose it does. But it's the easiest way of getting it to you quickly.

ELIJAH It's a pity someone can't invent a way of freezing food and transporting it safely.

GOD [*slowly*] Ah, well! It's funny you should say that, for one day—

ELIJAH [*interrupting*] But in the meantime, I give the king your message, disappear to Cherith, and wait for the ravens to produce food.
[*Sighs*]
Well, I suppose no-one said that the life of a prophet would be easy!

115

41

Solomon's choice

2 Chronicles 1.7–12

GOD	Solomon, are you awake?
SOLOMON	[*more asleep than awake*] What? What's that?
GOD	Are you awake?
SOLOMON	[*crossly*] Am I awake? What a silly question! If I wasn't awake a moment ago, I certainly am *now*!
GOD	[*amused*] That's true.
SOLOMON	Anyway, who on earth wants me at this time of the night? [*Suddenly wide awake*] I thought I gave orders that no-one was to disturb me? It's been a long, hard day travelling all the way to Gibeon with most of the army—
GOD	[*interrupting*] Never mind spending the day in worship, and the sacrifice of a thousand animals!
SOLOMON	[*remembering*] Too true. The heat was like nothing I've ever experienced before. [*Amused*] There were men going down like flies with the heat from the sun, never mind the heat from the sacrificial fires laid on the altar.
GOD	It was quite something to watch.
SOLOMON	It certainly was, but then we have a lot to thank God for.
GOD	I'm glad to hear it.
SOLOMON	[*remembering his grievance*] Anyway never mind that! What on earth do you think you're doing waking me up! I'd just managed to get to sleep.

	[*Sulkily*]
	Now it'll take me ages to get back.
	[*Another thought*]
	And how did you get in here? Where's the guards? I'll have their heads for this – can't even sleep in peace after a long day.
GOD	[*apologetically*] I'm very sorry, Solomon. I just thought it would be good to talk.
SOLOMON	Good to *talk*?
GOD	Well, there wasn't much time during the day was there? Too much noise, too much fuss, too much of everything to really speak to one another.
SOLOMON	And what makes you think I *want* to speak to you?
GOD	[*surprised*] I thought that was the purpose of the whole activity today.
SOLOMON	[*laughing*] To speak to you? Don't make me laugh!
GOD	[*genuinely interested*] So what was the purpose of today?
SOLOMON	To speak to *God*, of course.
GOD	[*dryly*] Exactly!
SOLOMON	[*long pause, then a gulp*] God? Is that you speaking?
GOD	I'd like to know who you think might be sneaking into your bedchamber at this time of the night!
SOLOMON	[*embarrassed*] It's just I wasn't expecting you.
GOD	[*dryly*] So what on earth was the purpose of today if you didn't want to speak to me?
SOLOMON	[*awkwardly*] I mean I didn't expect you to come and speak to me personally.
GOD	Oh, well that's a change, most people want something from me when they start sacrificing on such a scale. Well done!
	[*Pause*]
	[*Changing the subject*] If I offered you a gift, what

117

	would you like me to give you? What if I offer you anything you want – gold, women, jewels, more land?
SOLOMON	[*pausing to think*] Are you serious?
GOD	Of course! I don't make such offers to everyone, you know!
SOLOMON	[*thinking fast*] You've always supported my father, David, and now you support me. Indeed you've made me king over all your people—
GOD	[*interrupting*] So, what would you like?
SOLOMON	I'm not sure.
GOD	There must be something you'd like.
SOLOMON	Oh, there is! [*Suddenly making up his mind*] I would ask you to give me wisdom. Make me wise enough to rule over all these people that you have given me. Without wisdom and knowledge I shall make a very poor king.
GOD	Well done, Solomon, you have chosen well. I could have given you long life, or wealth, but you have asked for wisdom and knowledge to rule my people. [*Pause*] I shall grant your request! And because you have asked for nothing for yourself, I shall give you something else. I shall give you great wealth and fame.
SOLOMON	I really don't know what to say, God.
GOD	And remember, Solomon, I *am* always here when you call.

42

Solomon and the Temple

2 Chronicles 6–7

SOLOMON   God?

[*Pause to listen*]

God?

[*Pause*]

Did you get my message? Not the one I sent this morning, but the one early yesterday morning?

GOD   [*wearily*] I do get rather a lot of communications from you, Solomon.

SOLOMON   [*humbly*] Sorry, God.

GOD   Which one are we talking about?

SOLOMON   It was about the Temple.

GOD   [*snorting*] About the Temple! They're *all* about the Temple. You've been sending me communications for months about the Temple. When have you sent anything else?

SOLOMON   Well, it has rather been on my mind a lot recently.

GOD   [*dryly*] I had noticed!

SOLOMON   Well, did you get it?

GOD   [*somewhat preoccupied with other thoughts*] What, what?

SOLOMON   [*peeved*] The message I sent yesterday about the Temple.

GOD   Was this the one about the pans for carrying live coals, or the golden lamps?

SOLOMON   [*still peeved*] Neither. It was about, well, it was about, well, *you*.

119

GOD   [*surprised*] Me! What have I got to do with all this? You're building the Temple, not me!

SOLOMON   Yes, I know. But I'm building it for *you*.

GOD   True.

SOLOMON   And well, I wondered, if, well, if you, might—

GOD   [*impatiently*] Oh, come on, Solomon, it's not like you to be shy. What is it you want?

SOLOMON   Well, I know that you are a God who lives in the clouds, who does not dwell in caves or in water. You inhabit the secret places – the places we have never seen – and you are bigger than our whole world.

GOD   [*impatiently*] Yes, yes. Get on with it!

SOLOMON   Now I have built a Temple for you – a place where you can live.

GOD   For me to *live*?

SOLOMON   [*continuing as though God has not spoken*] My father, David, planned to build the Temple in Jerusalem, and now I have completed the work. The Temple is where the people will worship you. It will also hold the stone tablets you gave to Moses – when you made the covenant with your people.

GOD   But why should I wish to *live* in this Temple?

SOLOMON   God, your people need to speak to you. We need you to watch over us and care for us. When we cry to you, hear our words. Let this Temple be somewhere we can come and ask your help – when the crops fail, or war threatens – here is where we shall come to ask your forgiveness.

GOD   [*pause*] I understand your request, Solomon, and I have seen the magnificence of the Temple.

SOLOMON   Then agree to my request, Lord. Let my Temple be a place for sacrifice and prayer where all your people may come to worship you.

GOD	It shall be as you ask. But be warned—
SOLOMON	[*interrupting*] Anything, Lord, anything!
GOD	—when the locusts destroy your crops, or the rain ceases, your people should remember their promise.
SOLOMON	What promise is that, Lord?
GOD	I shall be their God, and they shall be my people. If they obey my laws then I will protect them, but if they do evil—
SOLOMON	They will come to the Temple and repent—
GOD	[*pause*] Then I will hear them.
	[*Pause*]
	And I will forgive them.
	[*Pause*]
SOLOMON	So we may make our sacrifices in the Temple, and you will hear us?
GOD	I will watch over the Temple, and I will keep it safe. But heed this warning – I will abandon it if you and your people abandon me! Keep faith with me and all will be well.

43

Job repents

Job 3 and 38

JOB	God! Where are you? Don't try and hide from me! Why did you bother to let me live, you might as well have killed me at birth!
	[*Pause*]

121

Are you there? *Come on* don't try to hide!

[*Pause*]

Why do you let me live in such misery? Put an end to my life!

GOD   What is all this *caterwauling*?

JOB   [*furiously*] Caterwauling!

GOD   I've never heard such an awful noise!

JOB   Awful noise!

GOD   I do wish you wouldn't keep repeating everything I say, Job. It does get a little monotonous.

JOB   [*almost speechless with fury*] Repeating everything you say—

GOD   You see what I mean. You keep repeating—

JOB   [*interrupting*] Repeating everything you say! I should think I do!

GOD   There you are, you've done it again!

JOB   [*apoplectic*] Will you keep quiet for a minute! How on earth can I make myself heard!

GOD   [*dryly*] I rather thought you *were* making yourself heard—

[*Pause*]

[*Provocatively*] —caterwauling.

JOB   [*almost speechless*] But, but, my chil—

GOD   For goodness sake, what is the matter?

JOB   [*taking a deep breath, and trying to speak calmly*] My children are dead, my sheep destroyed, my camels killed – and you say I'm caterwauling?

GOD   [*positively*] Exactly!

JOB   [*overacting*] Why didn't you let me die? What point is there in living?

GOD   Quite a lot I would have thought, really. You have known much love in your life, Job, and much joy. Haven't you?

JOB   [*side-tracked*] Yes, I have. My daughters – they are so beautiful—

[Remembering]
Oh, my daughters! How will I ever live without them?

GOD   You will manage.

JOB   *[not listening to God]* Caterwauling, indeed! My whole world has fallen apart – my children dead, and all my wealth gone! Why have you done this to me, God?

GOD   Who are you, Job, to question me?

JOB   But why *me*, God? *Why me?*

GOD   How dare you! *Man*, you forget yourself!

JOB   *I* forget myself? *You* destroy my whole world and make complaint against *me*!

GOD   I say again, Job, who are *you* to question me? Are you not one of my creations? Am I not God, who made all things?

JOB   Of course you are! But if you create, why have you destroyed?

GOD   *[ignoring him]* Were you there when I made the world? Were you there when earth separated from the seas?

JOB   Of course not.

GOD   Did you create the stars or the heavens? Where were you when I commanded light to appear?

JOB   I wasn't born, as you know.

GOD   Do you know when the mountain goat needs food, or when the lioness will have her cubs? Will you provide rain for man to drink, and care for the raven and her mate?

JOB   You know the answer, God.

GOD   *[majestically]* Then who are you, man, to question me? Tell me! Who are you to question God?

JOB   Forgive me, God! I was only thinking of my own grief. I spoke without thought. Forgive me!

GOD   H'm.

JOB   My words were rash. I spoke of things I did not understand. My heart ruled my head, and you were right, I was caterwauling.

GOD   Your grief was understandable, Job, but your questioning was not.
[*Pause*]
However, the rest of your life will be lived in peace and prosperity, and my blessings will be upon you. Go in peace, Job!

44

What did you say, God?

Psalm 139

WOMAN   God?

GOD   Yes ——— [*adds Christian name of the woman*]

WOMAN   Are you there, God?

GOD   Of course I am. I'm always here, aren't I?

WOMAN   Are you? Well I'm not so sure about that. What about the time when my Dad fell and broke his leg? Where were *you* then?
[*Suddenly remembering other calamities*]
Oh, yes, and that time all the sheep escaped and we spent two days searching for them! You didn't seem to be around then, just when we needed you!

GOD   But I was there. I was also there when you became ill and the doctors gave up hope that you would survive.

WOMAN   A lot of good that was. I had to take weeks off work. What's the good of being with me if you don't do anything to help?

GOD   And whose fault was it that your father fell down and
          broke his leg, or that the sheep escaped?
WOMAN   [*thinking about the question*] OK, you're right it wasn't
          your fault. Dad fell over a box some idiot put on the
          stairs; and as for the sheep, well, someone left the gate
          open.
GOD   ———— [*name of woman*] I have been with you since
          before you were born. I know your thoughts and your
          dreams, your hopes and your fears. I will be with you
          wherever you go and whatever you do. There is
          nowhere you can go where I will not be with you!
WOMAN   [*sarcastically*] Well that's very nice of you, I'm sure, but
          what good is it if you can't stop me becoming ill?
GOD   [*gently*] Did you ever *ask* me for help?
WOMAN   [*thinking*] Well, I did ask—
          [*Being suddenly honest*]
          All right! I know I don't often turn to you, but I did ask
          for help when I was ill – and you weren't much help
          then. I nearly died!
GOD   But you didn't *die*, did you?
WOMAN   [*pausing to think*] No, I survived. My friend Mary died.
          But *I* survived!
GOD   So?
WOMAN   So you *are* with me and you *do* care for me?
          [*Suddenly taking it all in*]
          Heh, that's great!
          [*A sudden thought*]
          Hang on a minute, if you're always with me, that means
          you're with me when I, well, you know—
GOD   You mean, when you're up to no good?
WOMAN   Well, I wouldn't put it quite like that—
GOD   Wouldn't you? Perhaps you'd prefer the word *sin*?
WOMAN   Yes, well, you know what I mean. There are some times

125

when I'm not sure I really want you to be with me. It might be a bit uncomfortable.

GOD Exactly!

WOMAN But I suppose I can't expect you not to be there when I'm up to mischief, but at other times demand your help? After all you've got an investment in me, haven't you?

GOD I can't say I've ever thought of it quite like that!
[*Changing the subject*]
Anyway, what was it that you wanted, after all?

WOMAN Oh!
[*Pause*]
I can't remember!
[*Pause*]
But now I know that you are *always with me*, I'll come back to you when I need you.

GOD I'm sure you will ——— [*name of woman*]. I'm sure you will!

45

Warning against the women of Jerusalem
Isaiah 3.16–26

GOD [*calling*] Woman! Are you listening to me?

WOMAN I'm here.

GOD Then listen to this warning.

WOMAN   What warning?

GOD   [*irritated*] The one I am about to give you, of course!

WOMAN   [*pause*] Who are you?

GOD   [*baldly*] The Lord, your God.

WOMAN   [*laughing*] Pull the other one – 'The Lord your God'.
[*Goes off into howls of laughter*].

GOD   Woman!

WOMAN   [*still laughing*] What, *my Lord*? What can God want with me?

GOD   A warning, woman!

WOMAN   Oh, warn away! I'm always being warned – 'be careful or you'll get yourself into trouble'; 'watch what you're doing or something nasty will happen'. In fact my mother-in-law never stops warning me. So warn away!

GOD   This warning is for you and for all your sisters in Jerusalem – all the women of Jerusalem who walk so proudly through the streets.

WOMAN   Oh, it's not enough that *I get warned*, now you're warning *all* women. You don't want much, do you?

GOD   [*sternly*] Take heed that you are not so proud of your necklaces, your bangles, and your brooches. Take heed!

WOMAN   Charming! What's wrong with our jewellery?

GOD   Take heed that you do not care so much about your fashionable clothes or the magic charms you wear on your wrists or waists. Take heed!

WOMAN   Well, of all the nerve!

GOD   A time will come when all these shall be removed. A time will come when you will wear rags and you will be bald. Take heed!

WOMAN   What nonsense you do talk. Be bald, indeed! What on earth is all this about? Explain yourself.

GOD   Be warned!

WOMAN   [*crossly*] Stop this 'be warned' nonsense. Who are you,

	and what are you going on about? And how dare you threaten me!
GOD	I am the Lord—
WOMAN	[*interrupting, sarcastically*] —*your* God! I *know*! [*Pause, then realising*] Hang on! You mean you really are, God, I mean—
GOD	As I said.
WOMAN	I know you said so. But I thought you were joking. [*Pause*] Wait a minute, start again. Who is this warning for?
GOD	The women of Jerusalem.
WOMAN	And a time is coming when— [*Not wanting to say it*]
GOD	You will smell, your bodies will stink, you will wear rags and live off the rubbish in the streets.
WOMAN	[*aghast*] *All* of the women of Jerusalem?
GOD	All those who are left.
WOMAN	All who are *left*?
GOD	Your menfolk will all die in war, and my holy city, Jerusalem, will be stripped of all its beauty.
WOMAN	[*aghast*] Forgive me, God, but—
GOD	[*interrupting*] —My children have rebelled against me. They have ignored my warnings, worshipped other idols, and turned away from me.
WOMAN	But if we'd only *known*.
GOD	I have warned my people again and again. Now the time is late, and my anger burns brightly.
WOMAN	[*hurriedly*] What can I do to make amends, Lord God?
GOD	Repent and be forgiven.
WOMAN	[*desperately*] I do, God, I do! Forgive me!
GOD	And warn your sisters.
WOMAN	I will, immediately, God!
GOD	The hour is late and retribution is about to be de-

manded. Women of Jerusalem I am waiting to punish you! Be warned, and turn from your sins!

46
Jeremiah is given authority
Jeremiah 1.4–10

JEREMIAH   [*to himself, angrily*] I'm fed up! Why is it always me? Why can't someone else tell the people to change their ways. They never listen to me, anyway. It's not fair! Why can't someone else put their head in the noose? It's always me that gets it in the neck. They'll start calling me 'Jeremiah Jinx' soon.

GOD   [*amused*] Can anyone enter this conversation, Jeremiah? Or is it a private one?

JEREMIAH   Well, you may laugh at me, God. It's all right for *you*. You're not down here getting into difficulties every five minutes.

GOD   What's the matter now?

JEREMIAH   I'm fed up!

GOD   [*slightly amused*] Well, this sounds serious. Anything I can do to help?

JEREMIAH   [*indignantly*] Anything *you can do*? I should jolly well think there is! You can find someone else to speak to the people. Why does it always have to be me?

GOD   Because I chose you!

JEREMIAH   [*still indignant*] Well that's not an answer! What kind of answer is '*I chose you*'?

129

GOD	[*continuing*] I chose you before you were born. I appointed you to be a prophet – to speak to the people of Israel.
JEREMIAH	But did you ever *ask* me if I wanted to speak to the people?
GOD	I selected you for this work.
JEREMIAH	But you didn't *ask* me!
GOD	I could hardly do that before you were born!
JEREMIAH	Oh, great, now you're laughing at me! Very funny!
GOD	[*suddenly serious*] Jeremiah, what *is* the matter?
JEREMIAH	I can't do the job. I don't know what to *say*!
GOD	Have I ever asked you to think up your own speech? Have I ever asked you to think for yourself?
JEREMIAH	No, I suppose not.
GOD	Go to the people and tell them what I command you to say. Don't change anything. I will give you the exact words that you are to say.
JEREMIAH	[*relenting*] Well, that sounds a little better. But they're not going to like your words, are they?
GOD	[*dryly*] Probably not.
JEREMIAH	And it's always the messenger that gets hurt, never the one who sends the message!
GOD	You need not be afraid.
JEREMIAH	That's fine for you to say, you don't have to stand up to the people in the market place, or even worse, at court.
GOD	You need not be afraid. I *will* be with you.
JEREMIAH	You haven't seen the women down by the well. If they get angry they'll throw anything that comes to hand. A right vicious lot they are!
GOD	I will protect you.
JEREMIAH	[*not listening*] And as for standing outside the Temple, well, that's absolute suicide.

GOD   I will give you authority over all the people – and over
             all nations. You have the authority to pull down and
             destroy; or to build or to plant new nations.

JEREMIAH   [*suddenly hearing what is being said*] What was that
             you said?

GOD   I am giving you authority over all people – over all
             nations.

JEREMIAH   But everyone will be against me, everyone will seek to
             destroy me.

GOD   They will not hurt you, for I shall be with you to
             protect you.

JEREMIAH   [*giving in*] I guess I can stand against them all, then, if
             you are with me. For who offers greater protection
             than God?

GOD   *And* I will give you the courage to speak out, to give
             my people one last chance.

JEREMIAH   [*resigned*] Give me the words, then, that I may go and
             speak!

47

The odd request

Jeremiah 13.1–11

GOD   Paging Jeremiah! Paging Jeremiah! Call for Mr Jere-
             miah! Mr Jeremiah, are you there?
             [*Pause*]
             Ah, Mr Jeremiah, a word for you!

JEREMIAH   Yes, who is it? This is Jeremiah.

GOD	This is God, Jeremiah.
JEREMIAH	Ah, yes, God. What can I do for you?
GOD	I have a job for you to do.
JEREMIAH	You do? What is it?
GOD	I want you to go and buy some shorts.
JEREMIAH	[*pause*] Some *shorts*?
GOD	Some shorts – linen shorts to be precise.
JEREMIAH	Some *linen shorts*?
GOD	Yes, haven't I said so already?
JEREMIAH	Where am I to find some linen shorts – it's winter in Jerusalem, you know!
GOD	I'm sure you'll find them if you look. Somewhere is bound to sell them.
JEREMIAH	[*indignantly*] Linen shorts, indeed!
	[*Pause*]
	And what am I supposed to do with them when I find these linen shorts?
GOD	Put them on, of course!
JEREMIAH	Oh, of course, put them on! Indeed, what else should I do with a pair of shorts, in the middle of winter?
GOD	Make sure that they fit, then, won't you?
JEREMIAH	Well, they won't fit until they're washed, will they? You know what linen's like – it needs to be shrunk first.
GOD	No, on *no* account wash them first! They must not be put into water. Do you hear me?
JEREMIAH	[*as though humouring a small child*] Of course I hear you – don't put them into water before wearing them. Though what good that will be, I don't know!
GOD	You will see. Just have patience, Jeremiah.
JEREMIAH	[*to himself*] Sometimes I *need patience*, believe me!
GOD	Are you listening, Jeremiah?
JEREMIAH	Yes, God! So what happens then?

GOD	*Then*, I want you to take them to the river and find a hole to bury them in.
JEREMIAH	[*sarcastically*] Oh, sure! Put them on, don't wash them, and then bury them in a hole in the rocks by the river. Which river by the way?
GOD	[*patiently*] The River Euphrates, Jeremiah, where else?
JEREMIAH	[*flippantly*] Just wondered! I thought you might have another river in mind – a smaller one, maybe.
GOD	[*patiently*] Jeremiah, this is serious!
JEREMIAH	[*still sarcastic*] Of course it is, God – linen shorts, hidden in a hole. Very serious!
GOD	In a few days you are to go to the hole, and rescue the shorts.
JEREMIAH	What on earth for? They'll be ruined. They'll be no good for anything by then, the water and mud from the river will have totally destroyed them.
GOD	Exactly!
JEREMIAH	What do you mean, '*Exactly*'?
GOD	As I said, 'Exactly', they will be ruined!
JEREMIAH	But what is the point of this exercise? What will we have achieved?
GOD	Let us say that this is to teach you what will happen to the people of Israel.
JEREMIAH	What *do you mean*? I don't understand you!
GOD	My people were made to *cling* to me, like a pair of well-fitting shorts. But they have ignored my wishes and chosen other gods.
JEREMIAH	They have indeed!
GOD	My people are like the shorts left in the river bank. They are useless – they are good for absolutely nothing. [*Pause*] They will be thrown away and destroyed.

133

JEREMIAH	[*suddenly very serious*] Lord, give them one last chance!
GOD	[*sternly*] They have been given many *last* chances. Now you are to tell them I have spoken.
JEREMIAH	But, Lord—
GOD	Tell them! This is how I will destroy the pride of Israel! The time for warning is over. Do you hear me?
JEREMIAH	[*humbly*] Yes, Lord, I hear you. I will do as you have instructed, and I will tell the people of Israel what you have said.

48

Interpreting the king's dream
Daniel 2

DANIEL	I hope you're on form today, God, because if ever I've needed you, today's the day!
GOD	What? What's the matter now, Daniel? Have you ever known me let you down?
DANIEL	No, certainly not! You continue to amaze me, God.
GOD	So why the air of doubt, now, then?
DANIEL	It's the problem, really. It seems impossible to solve.
GOD	What problem? I thought everything was going well in the Babylonian court.
DANIEL	It was. Things were going amazingly well, considering.
GOD	In fact you seemed to have fallen on your feet, as I remember.
DANIEL	[*amused*] That's one way of putting it. My friends and I

have certainly landed on a feather bed. There's plenty to eat, a library to study in, teachers to educate us, and a whole palace to explore.

GOD Everything you could want!

DANIEL [*sighing*] Except for having to change all our names.

GOD [*astonished*] To change your *names*?

DANIEL Yes, didn't I tell you?

GOD No!

DANIEL Well, I'm now called Belteshazzar. What sort of name is that for a good Hebrew lad, I ask you?

GOD [*laughing*] I rather like it! It's certainly different. I bet you had problems getting your tongue round that name at first.

DANIEL [*amused*] I still do! Sometimes I forget when they call me, and think they want someone else.

GOD And what have they called Hananiah, Mishael and Azariah? I hardly dare to ask!

DANIEL Now wait a minute, I have to say these carefully. Their names are – Shadrach, Meshach, and Abednego.

GOD [*amused*] Sounds rather like a firm of tailors, don't you think?

DANIEL Or cobblers!

GOD Anyway enough of all this. What is the matter?

DANIEL We've just managed to avoid being put to death, that's the matter!

GOD Why are you to be put to death? What have you done?

DANIEL It's nothing we've done, it's rather what the Babylonians haven't done.

GOD [*confused*] What are you talking about?

DANIEL It's like this – Nebuchadnezzar, the king has had a number of dreams, and he can't get anyone to tell him what they mean.

GOD Couldn't his wise men help?

DANIEL   No. To be fair, the king asked them to interpret his dreams, without actually telling them what they were about.

GOD   Mean of him.

DANIEL   It was! Then, when they couldn't give him the answers he wanted, he ordered them to be killed.

GOD   But what has that to do with you? You're not one of his Babylonian sages.

DANIEL   Well, in a way we are. He's trained and educated us all these years so that we could join his group of advisers. So if they are to be executed, so will we!

GOD   Nice one, Nebuchadnezzar!

DANIEL   Never mind congratulating him. We need to find a way to get out of this.

GOD   Any suggestions?

DANIEL   Yes.

GOD   What are they, then?

DANIEL   We tell him what his dreams mean – if I can get near him without being caught by the guards first.

GOD   It might work.

DANIEL   It *has* to work, otherwise we're dead men.

GOD   So, how are you going to find out what he's dreamt?

DANIEL   [*as if talking to a small child*] I rather thought *you* might help!

GOD   Oh, I thought it might be down to me in the end! Nice to know I'm always needed ultimately!

DANIEL   Now don't be like that. You know perfectly well I can't manage without your help even for one day. Why do you think I spend so many hours talking to you?

GOD   All right! Here's what you need to know, then. Nebuchadnezzar dreams were all about—

49

Daniel asks God's help

Daniel 5–6

DANIEL   [*urgently*] God! Are you there? God! God! For goodness sake, answer me at once!

GOD   [*calmly, unhurriedly*] I'm here. What a noise!

DANIEL   [*to himself*] What a noise, he says, when I need him *now*!

GOD   I was rather busy, Daniel. You're not the only person in the world, you know. Now what is it?
[*Pause*]
Daniel?
[*Pause*]
Are you there?

DANIEL   I'm here!

GOD   Well, why didn't you answer me? I thought you'd disappeared.

DANIEL   No such luck! I just had to stop talking to you for a moment.

GOD   Oh, why was that?

DANIEL   [*very calmly*] I've got a slight problem.

GOD   Really?

DANIEL   Really!

GOD   [*slightly irritated*] Well, are you going to tell me about it, or shall I just guess?

DANIEL   [*small hysterical giggle*] Oh, I don't think guessing would be much good.

GOD   No?

DANIEL   You see, I'm a little pressed for time.

GOD   You are? Why?

DANIEL	I'm about to be eaten.
GOD	[*shocked*] What? Who by?
DANIEL	Three lions.
GOD	[*laughing*] Don't be daft! How could three lions get into the city. I hardly think King Darius would allow that to happen.
DANIEL	[*irritated*] It's no laughing matter. I'm in a lion pit, and if you don't hurry up and help me I'll be supper for three very hungry-looking animals.
GOD	But why are you in a lion pit?
DANIEL	Jealousy.
GOD	Jealousy? What's that got to do with being in a lion's den?
DANIEL	Darius, the king, appointed me, together with two other men to be in charge of his kingdom. But the other two are jealous of me and want to get rid of me.
GOD	And they used your faith to get at you?
DANIEL	Yes! They persuaded the king to send out an order that no-one in the kingdom is to pray to any god, other than to Darius himself.
GOD	And then they denounced you for worshipping me!
DANIEL	Yes!
GOD	But why a lion's den?
DANIEL	It's Darius' favourite form of execution.
GOD	Well, it saves him having to find food for the lions, I suppose.
DANIEL	[*sarcastically*] Very funny! If you don't get a move on, I'll be feeding the lions!
GOD	Now don't get in a panic. I hear you! I hear you!
DANIEL	I'm glad about that. I began to wonder if you were busy elsewhere.
GOD	As if I'd leave you alone, Daniel. You know better than that.

DANIEL	Then hurry up and get me out of here.
GOD	[*taking a decision*] No, I don't think I will.
DANIEL	[*in horror*] What? Get me out of here!
GOD	No, it would be far more effective if I left you in the den for the night.
DANIEL	Effective for whom? Not me, I think!
GOD	Effective for you too.
DANIEL	Not unless you want to get rid of me!
GOD	No, no, Daniel. I don't mean you to be killed.
DANIEL	[*with relief*] I'm glad about that. I began to think I might need to revise my thoughts about you, God.
GOD	Don't worry about the lions. They won't harm you.
DANIEL	Are you *sure*? I'd hate you to be wrong, you know.
GOD	And when have you known me to be wrong, Daniel?
DANIEL	Not often, I admit.
GOD	Not *often*?
DANIEL	Well, all right, *never*!
GOD	That's better. Now, here's the plan. In the morning when the king comes down to look in the pit, you will be alive.
DANIEL	And?
GOD	He will think that your God—
DANIEL	*You!*
GOD	*Me* – is a better God to worship than his own god.
DANIEL	And with luck I will be placed in charge of the whole kingdom! Brilliant! You've done it again, God!

50

Jonah changes his mind

Jonah 1–2

JONAH	God? Are you there?
GOD	As always! I'm here, and I'm listening! What do you want?
JONAH	[*puzzled*] Where am I? It's awfully dark and noisy here. And it smells!
GOD	Well, I'm not sure you're going to like this. Are you ready for a shock?
JONAH	I don't know. Will I like it?
GOD	I don't think so. In fact, I'd say, definitely not.
JONAH	[*not really listening, but thinking back*] The last thing I remember is—
JONAH/GOD	[*together*]—being thrown overboard.
JONAH	[*very worried now*] God, where exactly am I?
GOD	[*very matter-of-fact*] Inside a whale.
JONAH	[*shouting*] Inside a *what*?
GOD	A whale, you know, a large fish – swims in the sea and all that!
JONAH	[*slightly relieved*] Oh, come on! Don't muck about. This is serious. Where am I?
GOD	I told you – inside a whale.
JONAH	How did I get here?
	[*Suddenly realising what it means*]
	You mean I've been *eaten* by a whale?
GOD	Yep!
	[*Trying to make amends*]
	Although it's a very large one.

JONAH	[*still not taking it all in*] Swallowed, and *eaten*, by, a—
GOD	Whale.
JONAH	[*sudden thought*] But I'm still alive, aren't I?
GOD	[*dryly*] Very much so by the sound of it.
JONAH	Oh, thanks very much, that's just what I wanted – make fun of me!
GOD	[*mildly*] Well, you could be dead. It was rather a rough sea, and you were nowhere near land.
JONAH	And I suppose I've got to feel grateful, because I didn't drown?
GOD	Not at all. I never *expect* gratitude, though it's nice when it comes.
JONAH	Well, if it's all the same to you I think I'd like to get out of here—
GOD	That can be arranged.
JONAH	—preferably safe and sound!
GOD	Of course. [*Airily*] Now where was it you wanted to go?
JONAH	You know perfectly well. I was on my way to Spain.
GOD	Spain? Is that where you were going? I must have got it wrong. I thought you were on your way to Nineveh. Isn't that so?
JONAH	No! I've no desire to go to Nineveh. The people there are dreadful. They're all evil – as likely to kill you as to greet you!
GOD	I know.
JONAH	Well, of course you know. But really you could *do something* to sort them out. They're a disgrace to the Mediterranean.
GOD	[*mildly*] I rather thought I was trying to 'sort them out'.

141

JONAH	Were you? Well, you'd better try harder in future. They need destroying, like Sodom and Gomorrah! If you can do that to *those two* cities, why can't you get rid of Nineveh?
GOD	Not before I give them an opportunity to repent. I always do that.
JONAH	[*struck by the thought*] Do you? Yes, I suppose you do! Abraham asked you to keep Sodom and Go-morrah alive if he found ten faithful men in the city, didn't he?
GOD	Yes.
JONAH	Well, how are you going to give the people of Nineveh a chance to repent?
GOD	[*ironically*] I thought I'd already got that organised. Unfortunately it didn't quite work out.
JONAH	The trouble is that you're just not tough enough— [*Sudden thought*] Do you mean to say that I was supposed to give them their chance?
GOD	Er, precisely! Yes!
JONAH	Thank you very much! [*Another thought – somewhat amused*] And you were giving me a chance as well, I suppose.
GOD	Yes.
JONAH	Oh, great! Nineveh – or be swallowed by a fish! Well, you'll be pleased to know I've made up my mind, with a bit of help from the whale! I'll take Nineveh after all. [*Pause*] Perhaps I can help persuade the people of Nineveh to accept life rather than death, having been given a choice myself. You win, God, as always!